REIMAGINING EDUCATIONAL LEADERSHIP IN THE CARIBBEAN

REIMAGINING EDUCATIONAL LEADERSHIP IN THE CARIBBEAN

Canute S. Thompson

With an introduction by Errol Miller

 The University of the West Indies Press
Jamaica • Barbados • Trinidad and Tobago

The University of the West Indies Press
7A Gibraltar Hall Road, Mona
Kingston 7, Jamaica
www.uwipress.com

© 2019 by Canute S. Thompson
All rights reserved. Published 2019

A catalogue record of this book is available from the National Library of Jamaica.

ISBN: 978-976-640-720-9 (print)
978-976-640-721-6 (Kindle)
978-976-640-722-3 (ePub)

Cover design by Robert Harris
Typesetting by The Beget, India
Printed in the United States of America

This book is dedicated to the memory of my parents,
Luther and Isolyn Thompson, both of whom introduced me to
different approaches to leadership.

Contents

Acknowledgements	ix
List of Abbreviations	xi
Introduction by Errol Miller	1
Chapter 1: Contextualizing the Task of Reimagining Educational Leadership in the Caribbean	7
Chapter 2: The Phenomenon of Postmodernism	13
Chapter 3: Leadership Approaches and Theories in Historical Perspective	27
Chapter 4: Proposition MRM	39
Chapter 5: Proposition MRM and Educational Leadership in the Caribbean	59
Chapter 6: Educational Leadership and the Future of the Caribbean	79
Chapter 7: A Concluding Word: Claiming a New Paradigm for Educational Leadership in the Caribbean	97
Afterword by Paula Shaw	99
Appendix: Students' Questionnaire: Students' Perceptions and Expectations of Leadership in a Postmodern Era	103
References	107
Index	115

Acknowledgements

I am deeply grateful to a few people whose input and support were vital in the completion of this publication.

I must first extend unending thanks to Professor Emeritus, the Honourable Errol Miller, a former director of the School of Education, regional icon and educator for the tremendous support he has graciously extended to me over many years in my academic journey and explorations in the field of education. I had the distinct honour of having Professor Miller serve on my panel of supervisors when I read for my PhD degree. I owe a great deal to Professor Miller for the quality of that work, which formed the base of a 2009 publication with the core findings being also used in this work. I am pleased and greatly honoured for the association of Professor Miller with this in the form of a foreword he has written. I wish to also express thanks to Professor Halden Morris, with whom I have had a long association, first as my research supervisor and for his review of this work.

Secondly, I wish to place on record my appreciation to the Ministry of Education, Youth and Information, Jamaica, for the engagements we have had concerning this work and the commonality of perspectives which we share on the role of technical and vocational education and training (TVET). It is my hope that the extensive treatment that is given to the subject in the book will serve to support the implementation of the TVET policy and the taking of bold steps to integrate TVET in the general curriculum. The implementation of the New Standards Curriculum in 2018 is an important first step but there are other important policy, institutional, attitudinal and cultural shifts that will be required. I have sought to address some of these steps and shifts in this book.

Thirdly, I wish to recognize the invaluable contributions of a number of former and current faculty colleagues at the School of Education, and especially Professor Disraeli Hutton, Dr Mairette Newman, Dr Lorna Down and Dr Therese Ferguson, who read the early versions of the manuscript and offered exceedingly helpful suggestions. I am also deeply indebted to my friend, colleague and fellow director of the Caribbean Leadership Reimagination Initiative, Dr Anna Perkins, for her insightful suggestions.

I must also thank a mentor and friend Professor Stafford Griffith, former director of the School of Education, whose graciousness as a leader and gentle but persistent focus on productivity in research have provided the ongoing impetus to complete this book. I must also acknowledge the encouragement I have received from the dean of the Faculty of Humanities and Education, Professor Waibinte Wariboko. I recall, with deep gratitude, his comments at the launch of my third book when, after commending the work, spoke to the need for me to focus attention on a "major" publication. That effort remains a "work in progress" but this book is a step towards that end.

Finally, I must thank my wife for the various ways in which she supports my work and efforts and in particular her contributions to the early phases of this work. I wish also to celebrate the constancy of her love as well as the encouragement of our three children. Their loving and undemanding ways of engaging and the space they allow for me to be often writing as well as their graciousness and patience are major contributors to my health and well-being.

Abbreviations

CEO	chief executive officer
EQ	emotional intelligence
ICT	information and communication technology
IMF	International Monetary Fund
MRM	modelling, respect, motivation
OECD	Organization for Economic Cooperation and Development
SD	sustainable development
TVET	technical and vocational education and training
TQM	total quality management

Introduction

ERROL MILLER

Dr Canute Thompson was one of those doctoral students that supervisors delight to have. Self-motivated with a voracious appetite for surveying and reviewing literature, there was never the need to urge him to get on with the work. The opposite was true. It was always challenging to keep up with his pace, given one's other commitments. Possessed of strong analytical skills, there was never any hold-up with research design, data collection, analysis of data, reporting findings and drawing inferences. Moreover, Dr Thompson was never one to follow the beaten path but was always probing and testing the unknown and untried with independence of mind. It is therefore not at all surprising that he is now advancing in the academy as a leader engaged in thinking through Caribbean realities.

Central to the book is the fact that Dr Thompson shares the main findings of his doctoral research with a wider audience and in a broader context than the requirements of a postgraduate credential. While the original findings from this research focused on the perceptions of Jamaican high school students of their principals, he has expanded upon his analysis of the findings of this work extensively and in a systematic form around his novel contribution: proposition modelling, respect, motivation (MRM). His treatment of this issue in chapter 4 is exciting and inviting. The claim is that Proposition MRM is a new interpretation for transformational leadership which he has refocused to inform a new approach to educational leadership in the Caribbean. Dr Thompson has the knack of rescuing, restoring and refreshing concepts, which, over time and because of common usage, have departed from their essential meaning.

The most controversial element of the book is the discourse on postmodernism. Indeed, anyone interested in a quick overview of postmodernism, point and counterpoint, will find the discourse in chapter 2 informative. While there is no doubt that Dr Thompson is an advocate, or at least an apologist, of postmodernism, he has come to this position fully cognizant of its tenets as well as criticisms of those tenets.

Reimagining Educational Leadership in the Caribbean is well written in a style of gushing prose, which rushes across wide expanses of thought. For example, in discussing the dogmatism that is said to characterize a fundamentalist world view, the text states: "One implication of this new dynamic and its relevance to pedagogy is that students enter a world that is crafted on diversity, characterized by ambiguity, propelled by plurality and steeped in complexity with an orientation to reject prefabricated postulations which are deemed to be out of sync with the realities around them" (p. 62).

Accordingly, the book has to be read with constant reflection on what is being stated if one is not to be swept away and mesmerized by its eloquence.

Fundamental axioms of the book are that current Caribbean realities are best depicted as a postmodern era, as is the case of western Europe and North America, and that postmodernism ought to be the guiding construct in pondering leadership in education and management. By fully asserting these axioms, setting them out in such clear terms and proposing approaches in their application, Dr Thompson has thrown down the gauntlet challenges his readers and colleagues to be equally clear and decisive about the constructs employed in thinking, writing and work as these are focused on the Caribbean.

There are numerous conceptual schemes that have been used to depict and interpret the history of civilization and social thought. From a technological perspective, human civilization and society can be traced from the primordial hunter-gather stage through the agricultural revolution, to the revolution in agricultural productivity, to the industrial revolution and now the information revolution. From a political perspective, human civilization could be said to have moved from ethnocentric villages based on subsistence agriculture, to the era of ancient city states premised on citizenship, to the era of imperial city-state empires, to the era of religious empires of believers and to the current era of nation-states of nationals and aliens. In a sense the conceptual scheme of premodern, modern and postmodern condenses elements of both technological and political schemata.

If one accepts the conceptual scheme of premodern, modern and postmodern, it is extremely difficult to conceive of Caribbean societies as anything other than modern. There are different markers that have been used in dating the modern era. The earliest is the scientific revolution of the first half of the seventeenth century as Europe emerged from the period, labelled medieval, which was dominated by religion. The latest dating is from the latter half of the nineteenth century when nation-states of the West confronted the challenges of industrialization, urbanization and representative democracy. Sandwiched between these early and late dates is the "Age of Enlightenment", beginning in the latter half of the eighteenth century. Whatever marker is chosen, Caribbean societies fit the timeframe of modern. Colonialism ensured that. In the seventeenth century, rising imperial nations of western Europe brought their newly established Caribbean colonies into the same status as themselves.

Common criteria that have been used to define modernity include representative democracy, public education, capitalist market economy, civil service bureaucracy and notions of freedom, individualism and equality. Representative democracy in the Commonwealth Caribbean evolved in sync with Britain itself. Barbados has had an elected assembly that has operated continuously since 1639 with the holding of general elections as prescribed by its constitution. Similarly, Jamaica has held general elections, with the exception of eighteen years, since 1661. The creation of the sugar plantation economy ensured that Caribbean colonies were part of capitalist market economies since the latter half of the seventeenth century. As Higman (2008) pointed out, plantations were privately owned agro-industrial operations which not only grew sugar cane and timber, but generated their energy by wind, or animals or water, and manufactured sugar, rum and molasses mainly for export from ports, many of which they owned and controlled. Further, the entire operation required effective and integrated management, and, as Higman observed, Caribbean managers were on par or ahead of their peers in Britain.

Public education in the Caribbean dates back to the latter part of the seventeenth century and became more general following emancipation in 1838. The civil service in Jamaica was established about fifteen years after that in Britain and on the same basis of civil service examinations. Issues of freedom, equality and individualism have been part of Caribbean culture from at least the beginning of the nineteenth century. Whether by timeframe or common criteria defining modernity, Caribbean societies have been modern societies, although of lesser means.

Historically, by virtue of their colonial past, Caribbean countries were brought into the modern era. Now in the era of political independence, starting in the second half of the twentieth century, the facts of geographical proximity of the Caribbean to the United States and Canada, the great extent of two-way travel of peoples between North America and the Caribbean, the shared English language, the ubiquity and ease of telecommunication, and growing social media have ensured continuous connection of modernity, however it is conceived and defined.

Having considered the pros and the cons, Dr Thompson seems to have concluded that history, geography and information and communication technology have combined to tie the destiny of the Caribbean to be conceptualized by the same schema as the West, whether modern or postmodern. In a nutshell, postmodernism is a conceptualization that the Caribbean dare not ignore. The crucial question becomes whether Caribbean engagement with postmodernism should be one of embrace and application or one of deep critical assessment and alternative formulation. Either way, *Reimagining Educational Leadership in the Caribbean* is an important contribution to this conversation.

The concept of modernity implies superiority to what went before. Embedded is the notion that Western civilization, characterized by modernity, is not only superior to civilizations of the past but also to all other civilizations that exists in the contemporary world. Yet, postmodernism embraces the notions of decline, decadence and transition. It declares modernity to be obsolete. As Jurgen Habermas asserts, while there is still the unfinished business of modernity, there is transition to something new. Lyotard agrees but for a different reason. He maintains that modernity perpetuates the myth of human progress and entertains grand or metanarratives that have been found wanting and must be abandoned. Regardless of perspective, the term postmodernism is similar to terms of yesteryear such as post-primary and post-secondary. Postmodernity is a stage beyond modernity but cannot yet be defined in terms of itself because, as an emerging stage, it is too embryonic to be endowed with settled form and unambiguous definition.

If postmodernism is subjected to the tool of deconstruction, at least three critical issues immediately rise to the fore. First, postmodernism is a resisting form of affirmation of the superiority of Europe and of the West. Even in decline and decadence, postmodernism implicitly asserts that Europe and the West are ahead of the rest of the world, some parts of which are still to struggling to become modern. The destiny of the world is to follow Europe and the West. The stage into which modernity is transitioning will arise from within Europe and the West and not from elsewhere. Europe and the West are leaders forever. Applied to the Caribbean, this means that having transitioned from being colonies to being politically sovereign countries, there is no change in the relationship with the West.

The destiny of the region is to continue to imitate and follow the powers that have dominated the region historically and subordinated its peoples, even in their decline and decadence. Second, the failure of the grand and metanarratives of Europe and the West is not their failure alone. It represents the failure of all human kind. If they have failed to formulate theories that can explain the full range of human social complexities, then no others can. There is no originality of mind, creativity of spirit or authenticity of experience that can produce grand or metanarratives superior to the West, or that will advance understanding of human society beyond of the theorizing of the West. Third, Europe and the West bear no responsibility, and cannot be held accountable, for their stewardship of the power they exercised over the last three to four hundred years when they dominated the rest of the world. Further, since every society, culture and people are entitled to their own truth and facts, it is only the lived experience of the present that matters. There are no lessons to be learned from our colonial history and no inferences that can guide our present and future choices, save and except the dynamic forces at work in specific places in the contemporary world. We are all cornered, even in our thinking, in our small spaces on the globe.

Some of the issues outlined above manifest themselves as Dr Thompson applies postmodern constructions to education in chapter 5. In referring to diverse communities existing side by side, it is asserted that based on the tenets of postmodernism, there is no way to adjudicate the truth claims between communities in postmodern plural society. Truth is a social construct for the sake of maintaining power. "Claims for truth must be deconstructed to expose underlying agendas and grabs for power" (p. 81). Many questions immediately shout for answers. First, why should there not be multiplicity of truth claims within communities as exist among communities in plural society? Should not everyone, regardless of community, have same right to her or his own truth? Hence, every truth claim is a grab for power whether by an individual or by a collective of individuals, a community. Second, does not truth as a social construct favour the status quo, that is, current holders of power and whose truth claims prevail by whatever means: ballot, bullet or market forces? Third, in the absence of any objective basis to adjudicate truth claims, is everything not spin, including postmodernism? Fourth, based on this construction of truth, are plural societies not inherently anarchical? Is the mission of postmodern education, and its leadership, to foster anarchy?

This is just one example of the provocative substance of the book as it invokes the tenets of postmodernism. It is not possible to read this section and not furiously grapple with the issues posed almost on every page. By being so explicit in the assertion of postmodernism, Dr Thompson has done a great service by causing reflection on implicit adoption of several aspects of postmodernism that virtually go unnoticed and without debate. For example, in many research studies currently done in education and the social sciences, the major methodology of postmodernism is employed qualitative methods. This is often done without connection to their postmodern source. Rich insights gained by these methodologies are not limited and restricted to the particular case and circumstance but are then used to attempt to construct grand and metanarrative, which is in direct violation of one of the basic tenets of postmodernism and of qualitative methodology itself.

The reader is taken on a journey which includes the ideas of leadership of Sir Shridath Ramphal, Rex Nettleford and Michael Manley as these relate to the author's Proposition MRM. The author takes the reader on a tour of the main theories of leadership since the beginning of the twentieth century: scientific management, human relations, behavioural science and post-behavioural science seen as by-products of postmodernism.

One of the findings of Miller (1984), who tracked research findings that were translated into educational policy, programmes and practices, was that it was the movement of university researchers or their graduate students into policy or leadership positions that accounted for this outcome. With firm faith in their findings, these researchers turned policy advisors or policymakers, or principals or heads of departments took the real risks involved in translating research findings into policies, programmes and practices. Fear of failing students, clients and customers, or of losing their jobs, make those not intimately involved in the particular research much less sanguine about the efficacy and practicality of research results and therefore more averse to taking the risks related to implementation. The translation of research findings into policy, programme and practices is not an impersonal matter. It requires personal knowledge that often transcends what is written in research reports.

1 | Contextualizing the Task of Reimagining Educational Leadership in the Caribbean

Educational leadership may be defined as the behaviours, decision-making processes and modes of engagement that are undertaken to advance the socialization, training and development of youth for meaningful participation in the education system and the socio-economic endeavours of a country. Educational leadership therefore is reflected in the relationship between policymakers and practitioners at one level; representatives of policymakers and school leaders at another; school leaders and teachers at yet another level; and school leaders (including classroom teachers) and students, parents and members of the wider community at the other level. Thus, educational leadership occurs at the macro (sector-wide) and micro (institutional) levels and is concerned with the design and implementation of policies and programmes that govern the education sector and the operations of educational institutions and the relationships among stakeholders and participants within these contexts. Educational leadership is also reflected in the relationship and organizational arrangements among stakeholders in the educational enterprise, one the one hand, and donor agencies and external agencies and governments, on the other.

In this book, I explore the nature of the cultural phenomenon called postmodernism as well as the Proposition MRM construct with a view to examining their relevance to, and desired and possible impact upon, the practice of educational leadership. Postmodernism is a worldview that is seen as one of the latest cultural phenomena that is informing how the world is viewed and how reality is interpreted. Postmodernism has been variously described as a new era, a new epistemology, and one of the many "post" theories alongside ideas such as post-structuralism.

Proposition MRM refers to the constructs *modelling, respect* and *motivation,* and were derived from empirical research which sought to understand the major leadership expectations of students and is more fully described in chapter 4. My first exploration of Proposition MRM was in positioning it as a particular approach to, and definition of, transformational leadership. The exposition of these ideas is contained in a 2009 publication entitled *Towards Solutions: Fundamentals of Transformational Leadership in a Postmodern Era*. This approach to, and definition of, transformational leadership emphasizes the principles of egalitarianism, power sharing and inclusiveness, and proposes a broader interpretation of the concept of respect. These principles are advanced as representing key elements of the nature of leadership in a postmodern era. This book expands on the ideas contained in the 2009 publication and explores what postmodernism and Proposition MRM may mean for the practice of *educational* leadership.

Locating the Reimagination of Educational Leadership

By exploring what postmodernism and Proposition MRM may mean for the practice of educational leadership, I am essentially inviting the reader to engage in a reimagination of educational leadership. This invitation to reimagine educational leadership is predicated on the assumption that existing ways of conceiving of educational leadership are not effectual in the current contexts within which countries and education systems of the Caribbean operate.

Reimagination, as a mode of behaviour, involves an examination of strongly held and generally accepted notions of how things are, and deemed ought to be (Thompson 2013). This examination is predicated on the view that even that which appears functional may possess inherent weaknesses, and that there is no guarantee that what is working well today may continue to work well in the future (Thompson 2013). However, there is even a greater and more audacious reason for engaging in reimagination and it is that one has examined one's reality and has made the determination that existing in a different mode is an absolute necessity (Nettleford 1970).

In the earlier work, Proposition MRM is looked at through the prisms of egalitarianism, power sharing and inclusiveness. In this work, I seek to examine the implications of Proposition MRM for various elements of the educational enterprise such as pedagogy, applied learning, educational policy and sustainable development (SD). In exploring these issues, I present technical and vocational education and training (TVET) as an important vehicle of education in a postmodern era and a vivid application of Proposition MRM. By juxtaposing postmodernism and Proposition MRM, I am making the claim that the latter reflects the spirit and focus of the former and specifically that the characteristics of Proposition MRM are in many ways similar to the characteristics of postmodernism.

The critical underpinning of this work is its attempt to show the relevance of postmodernism and Proposition MRM for educational leadership in the Caribbean. In pursuit of this objective, this book undertakes a brief exposition of the basic philosophies of three Caribbean political and cultural icons who also were educational leaders at heart. This book explores points of commonality between the thinking of these three Caribbean icons and Proposition MRM, and sets out how the principles of Proposition MRM may be understood using the prism of these educational philosophers. The three thinkers are the former chancellor of the University of the West Indies, Sir Sridath Ramphal; the late principal of the University of the West Indies, Professor Rex Nettleford; and the late prime minister of Jamaica, Michael Manley. The justification for my selection of these three thinkers is discussed in further detail in chapter 4 where I explore the basic elements of their philosophical bents and show the alignment of their thinking to Proposition MRM. But the basic consideration for engaging these three thinkers is that Proposition MRM undertakes a critique of strongly held assumptions and is thus similar in some respects to the basic bent and trajectory of the intellectual leadership of Ramphal, Nettleford and Manley. I submit, therefore, that these three Caribbean icons had in various ways invited governments, educational leaders and educational practitioners of the Caribbean to *reimagine* educational leadership. In this regard, this work represents both a renewal of that call to reimagine educational leadership as well as a deposit in furtherance of the reimagination project.

Ramphal, Nettleford and Manley were major players in the shaping of aspects of the Caribbean's political ideology and personality, as well as contributors to the Caribbean's socio-economic superstructure, including the philosophical and sociological framework of educational policy in the Caribbean. All three were educational leaders (and educational philosophers) in their own right and exercised the courage to doubt and dispute the presumed legitimacy and absoluteness of the inherited Eurocentric narratives. They sought to define the Caribbean, and inevitably our economy, both sociologically and politically. All three also held to a strong disposition towards the marginalized and excluded and were champions of the ethic of community and egalitarianism. All three promoted the doctrine of a common and shared space called the Caribbean Community in which each citizen, regardless of ethnicity or country of origin, was expected to be treated as an equal member of the community. This book then explores some lines of continuity between Proposition MRM as a philosophy of inclusiveness, and a critique of the status quo, on the one hand, and the ideology of educational leadership of Ramphal, Nettleford and Manley, on the other.

Imperatives of Educational Leadership in the Caribbean in a Postmodern Era

In contemplating the imperatives of educational leadership in the Caribbean in a postmodern era, I have identified two areas that call for attention and which I have sought to explore in the body of the work. These areas are inclusivity and collective consciousness on the one hand and Caribbean epistemologies on the other. Both constructs are germane to the task of this work, which seeks to engage in a reimagination of educational leadership within the Caribbean context. As a foundational point, it is worth noting that imagination begins in the consciousness and thus reimagination involves a reexamination of consciously held perspectives and points of view.

Inclusivity and Collective Consciousness

The need for a collective consciousness emerges from the fact that each member of the school the community has the capacity to contribute meaningfully to the execution of its mission. Indeed, one of the claims of postmodernism is that knowledge has broken down of the walls of exclusion. With greater access to knowledge and consistent with the notion that justice means inclusion, and justice being a post-behavioural and postmodern virtue, leadership in all spheres, must seek to draw on the contribution of all stakeholders. What this means, in effect, is that educational leaders, whether at the micro level of the institution (led by the boards of management, the principals and classroom teachers), or at the macro or sector level, are called upon to devise new ways of ensuring that leadership and governance are more inclusive. The issue of inclusion has implications for both the preparation of students for their life's work and citizenship, as well as for the sustainability of the work of the educational institutions and the education sector.

This collective consciousness, being seen as a postmodern virtue and necessity, is related to the need for Caribbean societies to both develop the capacity to push back against the continuing hegemonic tendencies of the powerful nations and their desire to control the socio-economic dynamics of Caribbean countries. The need for this collective consciousness is also based on the objective to instil in Caribbean students the ethos of cooperation as part of the redefinition of Caribbean society, in contradistinction to the competition and isolation that have characterized Caribbean society both at the country and regional levels. This collective consciousness, which is not unlike that which is typical of some ethnic groups like the Jews, is defined by Sir Sridath Ramphal as the "WI (we) consciousness" (Ramphal 1997).

Thus, educational leadership in the Caribbean in this postmodern era must reckon more insightfully and creatively with the reality of the need to prepare students for the age of the threat of extinction. By this, I mean that with globalization existing side by side with postmodernism, there is the ever-present danger that the Caribbean will become absorbed and unidentifiable in a globalized world. Thus, educational leadership in the Caribbean should be focused on the need not to leave the thinking through of its identity and the determination of its destiny in the hands of those who for centuries have controlled the socio-economic foundations of the region. Educational leadership in the Caribbean should form the foundation of the culture of resistance against conscription, sublimation and eventually extinction. That process begins with the practice of inclusive leadership and continues with an ongoing agenda of collective consciousness.

Caribbean Epistemologies

There is an urgent need for Caribbean education to bring to bear on the global discourse about progress and developmental priorities an epistemology that takes greater account of the Caribbean reality. Such a discourse will have to be positioned as a counternarrative to the dominant perspectives that seek to determine the metrics of progress and the elements of development. These Caribbean epistemologies should be predicated on the principle of community, power sharing the affirmation of multiple paths to truth and economic progress, and the inherent value of the perspectives of the erstwhile marginalized. These proposed elements of Caribbean epistemologies reflect the core ingredients of postmodern thinking. In essence, therefore, the arrival of the postmodern era and what postmodernism means may be said to be conterminous with the emerging need for an approach to educational leadership that emphasizes the need for paths to knowledge that give space to those voices which were disregarded, but more importantly to design an approach to educational leadership that ensures that Caribbean students are prepared to advance epistemological perspectives that reflect their Caribbean reality.

The need for Caribbean educational leadership to be disposed towards fostering the development of home-grown, but globally relevant, epistemologies is informed by the fact that the Caribbean has been an inheritor and user of epistemologies that have been constructed by thinkers whose contexts and realities are radically different from that of Caribbean students. These epistemologies have shaped the narratives that define self-understanding, social arrangements and approaches to solving problems of Caribbean peoples. The Caribbean as a former dominated space, and its peoples and social arrangements that were inflicted and infected with narratives constructed by others, now needs to take stock of those narratives and engage in the radical deconstruction of existing narratives and paradigms and create contextual and inclusive counternarratives. It is against the backdrop of these two principal perspectives that I submit that the educational leadership enterprise in the Caribbean should be pursued.

2 | The Phenomenon of Postmodernism

KhosraviShakib (2010) argues that postmodernism is premised on the explicit and argued denial that grand theories and ideas are in and of themselves sufficient to explain the realities of modern society or even provide an explanation for ancient phenomena and human experience. He describes postmodernism as a cultural climate, intellectual position, political reality and academic fashion. Locating its increased momentum in the 1970s, KhosraviShakib contends that postmodernism's aesthetic is its struggle to make sense of fragmentation.

KhosraviShakib (2010) appears to agree with Anderson (1998), who argued that postmodernism is a cultural phenomenon, characterized by the challenging of convention, the mixing of styles, the tolerance of ambiguity, an emphasis on diversity, the acceptance and celebration of change and innovation, the redefining of paradigms, the embrace of intellectual plurality and the affirmation that reality is not primordial but constructed. It contrasts with fundamentalism, which is a form of resistance to intellectual and cultural pluralism.

Harvey (1990) locates the timing of increased momentum of postmodernism in the 1970s as suggested by KhosraviShakib. Harvey argues that its emergence was immediately post–World War II but became a movement in the 1970s. The term "postmodernism" first entered the philosophical lexicon in 1979, with the publication of *The Postmodern Condition* by Jean-François Lyotard. The notion of a postmodern *condition* as advanced by Lyotard (1979) is consistent with Harvey's articulation that postmodernism is a cultural phenomenon which has had a profound impact on contemporary society and its institutions.

Ironically, the age of postmodernism exists alongside the age of globalization. Postmodernism emphasizes cultural and intellectual diversity while globalization emphasizes integration and convergence. Globalization in this sense is a form of fundamentalism, as its basic intent is the reimposing of "order" on a fragmented postmodern world (Rapley 2004).

Postmodernism's post–World War II roots may have been watered by the relativists' arguments of the 1950s. Relativism as Baghramain and Carter (2015) explain is the view that truth and falsity, right and wrong, standards of reasoning, and procedures of justification are products of differing conventions and frameworks of assessment and that their authority is confined to the context giving rise to them.

The basic argument of relativism is that if one believes something then it is "real". Thus, the question concerning truth, according to the relativists, is not "What is true?", but "Whose truth?", or more politically, "How did this version of what is believed to be true come to dominate our belief system?" Thus, what I describe as the ethos of postmodernism represents a cultural reinforcement of relativism and, I would argue further, gives rise to the notion of constructivism.

In emphasizing the constructivist character of postmodernism, Sexton (1997) divides human history into three distinct eras: premodern, modern and postmodern. Each of these periods emphasized a particular ontological and epistemological perspective that shaped how people dealt with events, problems and solutions.

The premodern era spans the sixth century BCE through to the Middle Ages, roughly, and emphasized dualism, idealism and rationalism. Faith and religion played central roles. By comparison, the modern era spans the Renaissance to the middle of the twentieth century (though some thinkers suggest that the modern era ended its dominant influence in the nineteenth century). Modernist thinking stressed empiricism, logical positivism, scientific methodology and the identification of objective truth – which was obviously deemed to be external. The third era, postmodernism, spans the mid-twentieth century to the present and accentuates the *creation* (or construction) rather than the *discovery* of truth.

While there is some debate over whether postmodernism emerged in the nineteenth or twentieth century, the more compelling view suggests that it was first identified as a theoretical discipline in the 1980s, though it is not possible to determine a specific point in time at which *modernism* began to give way to *post*modernism.

Postmodernism's Challenge to Established Narratives

Rorty (1985) points out that "established" narratives – metanarratives – have entered the mainstream of social consciousness because those who tell them are the holders and inheritors of power. The upshot of the mainstreaming of metanarratives is that the dominant narrative comes to be recognized as the only correct way to view reality, thus reflecting the biases of those who promulgate them. The notion of established narratives suggests, for example, that the narratives on how school "ought" to be managed and how students "ought" to be taught reflect the narratives of those who had the power to impose their way on others and to give universal status to their personal narratives. In a postmodern world, the multiplicity of narratives and the variegated nature of truths are recognized. In this context, all narratives, whether they are leadership styles or pedagogical approaches, are open to debate and interrogation (Beck 1993).

Ultimately, this situation raises questions about the practice of governance, leadership, power and the arrangements pertaining to the structure of organizations and societies. It is against a background such as this that this book seeks to contribute to the question of how to organize institutions – and in particular, schools – in order to achieve the higher order priorities of education. These higher order priorities include the preparation of students for critical thinking and constructive engagement as shapers and influencers of the world in which they live. If the truth be told, many schools are doing a good job of preparing students for a world that no longer exists. As schools seek to prepare students for the new global realities, educational policymakers and practitioners must remain mindful of the fluidity and constantly changing environment.

Postmodernism is also responsible for the new emphasis on individuality and a customized approach to business and service delivery by virtue of its critique of universalism, mass production, mass broadcasting and the attempts to define experience through the narrow prism of those in dominant positions (Anderson 1998). Postmodernism emphasizes the "allowability" of free play and autonomy within the context of discourse towards finding solutions for the improvement of human society.

Postmodernism may, therefore, be applied to a wide-ranging set of developments in critical theory, philosophy, literature and culture, among others. It is generally understood as a reaction to, and an emergent trend from, *modernism*. *Post*modernism sits parallel to other schools of critical thinking such as feminism, communalism and democratic socialism, all of which are characterized by a hermeneutic of suspicion towards "metanarratives". This hermeneutic of suspicion rejects the grand, supposedly universal stories, theories and paradigms of gender and capitalism, that have defined culture and behaviour in the past, and have instead begun to organize life around a variety of more local and subcultural ideologies and myths.

Grogan (2004) describes the postmodern perspective as one which challenges educational leaders to guard against acquiescence to the system of standardization and instrumental metanarratives which leave little room for creativity and the construction of counternarratives. She emphasizes that avoiding this acquiescence carries a moral obligation, born in part out of the fact that educational leaders have agency – even if limited. Postmodernism which emerged as a discipline that sought to promote the concept of collectivity is applicable to pedagogy in that it emphasizes that students and teachers are in a collective learning enterprise. Postmodernism also promotes shared learning among students. Vygotsky (1978) found that when children are challenged to work on activities collectively and are encouraged to achieve what they are not capable of doing individually, learning takes place and development follows, thereby promoting higher cognitive processes which reduce competitiveness and selfishness.

The transformation of organizational leadership seen in the flattening of organizational structures and the creation and use of work teams and task forces set up to deal with specific organizational challenges is one of the many examples of a postmodern approach. In addition, greater involvement of the "ordinary" worker in decision making, increased emphasis on the right of every worker to be respected and the obligations of leadership to display agreed behaviours and be held accountable are among the more critical leadership elements of a postmodern outlook.

Many tertiary educational institutions have also been transforming their leadership and learning systems to take account of the developments in the landscape of leadership. These transformations have been promulgated by adult educators such as Bagnall (1994), Edwards and Usher (1995), and Briton (1996). Among the changes taking place at the tertiary level of education are more deliberate attempts to continuously improve the learning experience by making learning more relevant to the needs and realities of students and the expectations of the workplace.

The foregoing approaches and emphases (flatter structures, team-based solutions, continuous improvement, involvement in decision making, workers' rights and accountability) fall under the rubric of total quality management (TQM).

Postmodernism: A New Epistemology

Johnson and Duberley (2000) suggest that the consequence of a postmodern stance is that it postulates that attempts to systematically define or impose logic on events face a priori limits due to inherent fragmentation and subjectivity. Since epistemology is the science of how knowledge is justified, a postmodern epistemology essentially means ways by which we claim to come to knowledge must be suspect and all former ways by which knowledge is deemed to be acquired are in need of review and subject to critique. At the heart of what I would describe as the epistemological ethic are two fundamental questions: "How do we know that what we believe is true?" and "How do I go about discovering truth?"

Carson (1996) provides a good analysis of the epistemological disposition of postmodernism by placing in context the epistemological orientation of previous eras. He notes that *premodern,* which dominated the period of the Enlightenment (1200–1600) relied upon revelations of the supernatural. *Modernist* epistemology moved away from reliance on an all-knowing God to an autonomous self and found expressions in Descartes's *cogito ergo sum,* "I think, therefore I am." In modernist epistemology, truth is believed to be attainable if a rigorous method of searching for such truth is established. Once the methodological parameters are deemed credible, the knowledge that is produced was deemed to be true for all time, all contexts, all cultures and all peoples. The attainment of a universal truth status of knowledge that one uncovered, Carson notes, was the objective of a dissertation and was at the heart of the scientific method.

The epistemology of *postmodernism* moves away from the idea that it is possible to attain universal, timeless truth, and is content to affirm the subjectivity an relativity of knowledge, to question grand theories that made claims to universality, but more importantly, moves from and the Cartesian individualistic notion of "I" to what Tutu (2004) describes as the community principle of *ubuntu,* "I am because you are" or more delicately, "I am human because I belong."

Because knowledge is now more subjective, the scientific method is no longer deemed to be the only legitimate means by which relevant truth may be acquired and this has given rise to new approaches to conducting research and the birth of qualitative and mixed methods. Postmodernism affirms the multiplicity of truths in an embrace of otherness. The method of knowing that is consistent with the principles of postmodernism is not the abandonment, or the bracketing out, of previously highly esteemed sources of "truth" but the adding to the mix of other truths, other views, other beliefs and other perspectives. So, the distillation process becomes more nuanced, more complex and more time-consuming as there is far more material with which to work. This is in contrast to a premodern age where the grand theories were the only truths that were counted.

Faced with this kind of complexity, religious fundamentalists such as Grenz (1996) suggest that postmodernism is nothing more than a form of advocacy characterized by "gnawing pessimism". Fundamentalist thinking, as a form of resistance to pluralism, will understandably view postmodernism as pessimism as it will be felt that to question what has been held as true is to be pessimistic. In a somewhat similar vein, Fowler (1996, 179) seems to reduce postmodernism to a "loss of confidence in the foundational features of thought established by the Enlightenment". This view reflects the thinking that truth came from Europe, but more critically those who held power. While some conservatives such as Carson (1996) have written in support of the usefulness of postmodernism, other conservatives such as Padgett (1996) seek to dismiss it for its lack of what he calls "coherence". He insists that there is a large measure of truth in postmodernity, specifically its critique of modernity. Carson (1996) suggests that postmodernity is a helpful pendulum swing away from the "unnecessary dogmatisms and legalism of a previous generation" and adds that "postmodernity is waking us up to the fact that we have been canonizing our own interpretations for far too long".

Rather than representing a loss of faith (pessimism), postmodernism is an affirmation that Europe is not the only producer of knowledge. In this regard, postmodernism is an attempt at embracing many sources of insight and regarding other places as having capacities that are comparable to Europe's. Postmodernism is not so much a critique of the "what" of the insights of the Enlightenment but a critique of its claim of exclusivity and absolutism. While postmodernism may be a form of advocacy it is much more than that. If only a form of advocacy, postmodernism would be nothing more than a platform for defending its chosen issues and interests. But postmodernism is hardly a platform of defence, though broadly speaking it may be, but more crucially a platform of offence and critique. That postmodernism affirms that every point of view is open to critique does not represent pessimism; rather, it is a form of bold optimism and faith in the belief that the shapers of human society and its institutions can always improve and find better and more effective and relevant ways of dealing with the issues that confront them.

But while postmodernism may be deemed to represent the strongest assault yet on the claims of absolutism and exclusivity that were characteristic of the *grand theory,* assaults on absolutism are not new. Lyotard (1979), in the tradition of Ludwig Wittgenstein's critique of the possibility of absolute and total knowledge, argued that the various "master-narratives" of progress such as positivist science, Marxism and structuralism had failed and were defunct as methods of achieving progress. Some critics may argue that any discussion of structuralism, and indeed of postmodernism, without reference to Michael Foucault's work is incomplete. It is, however, to be borne in mind that while Foucault in his later works distanced himself from structuralism and though sometimes characterized as postmodernist, he always rejected the post-structuralist and postmodernist labels.

Foucault saw the need to develop a new approach to the search for knowledge but held that all truth is open to challenge even the assertion that all truth is open challenge! What Lyotard (1979) sought to do was not to advance an alternative grand theory but to propose that there are many truths and many paths to those truths, what Hoy and Miskel (1996) call equifinality. Lyotard's perspective (which is similar to that of other Europeans) was a critique of the European mindset in that it affirmed that there is no longer *one* truth but *many* truths.

A closer look at Europe generally would show, however, that the grand theory doctrine, while dominant, was being critiqued from within Europe itself well before the dawn of postmodernism. In the seminal Gifford Lectures on natural religion delivered at Edinburgh 1901–2, William James set out to "defend experience against philosophy" as being the real backbone of the world's religious life. The operative word here is *experience*. For centuries positivist thinking dismissed experience as being a relevant factor in "real science". (It was not until the emergence of feminism, black theology, liberation theology and other epistemologies and theories of the oppressed and marginalized were gaining acceptance as legitimate modes of inquiry that experience was given some form of credence.)

Thus, James's lectures, first published in 1902 under the title *Varieties of Religious Experience*, became an immediate bestseller and brought about a revolution by looking at religion not as it appeared in the object (God or the universe or revelation), but as it appeared in the subject (the believing, doubting, praying an experiencing person). The examples of religious thought and life chosen by James came from the widest variety of theological viewpoints – Muslim, Buddhist, Hindu, Jewish and Christian. James, in his provocative classic *A Pluralist Universe*, first published in 1909, was one of the earliest thinkers to advance a systematic point of view in defence of a pluralistic viewpoint. *A Pluralist Universe* represented the summation of his lectures on pluralism delivered as the Hibbert Lectures at Harvard in 1908 and sought to advance the "doctrine" of multiple truths and multiple paths (equifinality) to the truth. This notion of multiple paths to truth that was being advanced in 1909 may be characterized as pre-postmodernism thinking.

Durkheim (1979), in his *Elementary Forms of Religious Life*, like James in his pioneering thinking, seems to tend in the direction of acknowledging diversity and equifinality in the search for truth, though neither James nor Durkheim used the term "equifinality". Both James and Durkheim have influenced Knitter (1985) in his unorthodox and provocative book *No Other Name?*. Knitter, using both Jungian psychological theories and James's psycho-religious premises, has been successful in prodding debate on the issue of the multiplicity of truth and multiple paths thereto.

Keunzli-Monard and Keunzli (2004), in responding to criticisms that postmodernism is nothing more than a form of advocacy rather than a theory, argue that postmodernism is both a new epistemology (*postmodernism* – one word) as well as a new era, coming after modern – that is, *post*modern. They concede that this new epistemology is akin to other schools of thought such as Marxism and feminism, which are forms of epistemology. Postmodernism as a form of epistemology is based on various theories, such as constructivism, social constructivism and hermeneutics. The common ground of these theories is a post-positivist view of the world. The post-positivist view emphasizes the "constructedness" of reality stressing that reality is created and evolves in relationships. But while stressing the constructedness of reality, the trajectory of postmodernism's epistemology is also one of deconstruction.

The negative criticisms of postmodernism have also been handled by Rorty (1985) who, among other things, stresses that postmodernism's epistemology is based on a "hermeneutic of suspicion" and has as its primary motive an invitation to people to reflect upon the way they live and think.

Keunzli-Monard and Keunzli (2004) in making a qualified acceptance of the critique that postmodernism brought nothing new to the world argue that the statement is both true and false. They concede that it is partly true that postmodernism is a critique or a form of advocacy – as opposed to a theory – but insist that its intent is not to provide content but to question the ideas as they come from positivism and structuralism. They maintain, however, that it is wrong to affirm that postmodernism brings nothing new, as among the things it brought is an epistemological shift.

Postmodernism: A New Era

Bauman and Tester (2007) commenting on perspectives in the literature on postmodernism avers that the transition from modernism to postmodernism may be likened to a movement from "solid" (stable) times to "liquid" times (Bauman and Tester 2007). In strict terms, therefore, modernism and postmodernism may be likened to the shift from industrialization to post-industrialization.

One of the strong cases advanced in support of the view that postmodernism represents a new era as made by Anderson (1998), who posits that postmodernity is reflected in contemporary art, culture, economics and social conditions. These are the result of unique features of late twentieth and early twenty-first century life. These features include globalization, consumerism, the fragmentation of authority and the "commoditization" of knowledge. In previous eras, knowledge was gained by listening to, or reading the works of, "experts". In a postmodern era, knowledge has become a commodity and the power and pre-eminence given to experts has diminished as knowledge is everywhere. In a postmodern age, where truths are no longer the preserve of those with power, the search for knowledge no longer requires that we look to those with power to market and promote their positions, but we can look in many other places.

An even more compelling case in support of the view that postmodernism represents a new era has been made by Robertson (1992). In *Globalization, Social Theory and Global Culture,* Robertson (1992) sets out what he calls the phases of development. He identifies five phases or eras spanning the period 1400–1990.

Phase 1, the germinal phase, covered 1400 to 1750 and was characterized by the growth of new national communities, the widespread influence of Catholicism and new conceptions of the individual. The impact of Catholicism included a definition of truth as predetermined universal reality that was taught by those who had come to understand it, rather than involving a journey of discovery of multiple realities. It was this monolithic notion that James had sought to challenge.

Phase 2, 1750–1802, the incipient phase, was marked by emergent nation-states, international trade and the dominance of the West. Phase 3, 1870s–1920s, was typified by strong notions of modern ideals towards which societies should aspire, the emergence of global communications and the onset of global warfare (World War I). Phase 4 spanned the 1920s to the 1960s and consisted of the struggle-for-hegemony phase marked by conflicts between states for power and leadership in the world, the emergence of superpowers and growing poverty in the Third World.

The fifth era, phase 5, 1960s to the (then) present, bears many of the marks of the postmodern era as described in this book. These include the strengthening of local nationalism and the struggle for independence by many small states, increasing global cultural patterns and communication processes. The characteristics of phase 5 could be described in more detail to identify the growth of the rights movements, liberation theology, information technology and increased social diversity.

Postmodernism exists alongside other developments in human society and other equally valid forms of epistemology. Thus, this book does not claim that postmodernism is the only valid epistemology and that there is no other valid method of interpretation. As a social phenomenon its effects on human relationships and behaviours cannot, or ought not, to be studied as though no other phenomenon exists. Like all social phenomena, its impact cannot be measured discretely; however, there are identifiable behaviours which may be examined to determine the extent to which their existence is a product of the postmodern *spirit*.

Postmodernism and the Caribbean

Geofroy (2007) in examining the issue of Caribbean masculinity, contends that postmodernism provides an effective avenue for liberation as given its deconstructive mode, it allows for a redescription of what inherited reality, which even if generally accepted need not be seen as true. The assertion that postmodernism provides a path to liberation from oppressive gender or other constrictors is consistent with the claim of the postmodern construct which asserts that all social reality is negotiated (Berger and Luckman 1967). Geofroy contends that the ability to constantly engage in redescriptions could be harnessed in problem solving and holds the key to human progress. Thus, it may be argued that given the Caribbean's history of oppression a postmodern worldview is central to its liberation, which, Geofroy suggests, begins with redescription.

Geofroy's position is consistent with that of Berkeley (2012), who found in his critical appraisal of Phillips's (2007) work on multiculturalism that Phillips's benign linguistic genre obfuscates the reader's perception of social inequality. The suggestion here is that language is a critical tool in dealing with one's reality. The positions of Geofroy (2007) and Berkeley (2012) are supported by Thompson (2013), who incipiently affirms the importance of language and the need for redescription, and offers a more radically expressed notion of leadership reimagination.

Bailey (1998) looks at postmodernism through the opposite gender lenses and, in reviewing the literature on feminism and educational research, notes that as a result of the research work of feminists who are concerned with educational inequalities, three major sets of competing theories have evolved to explain the differential effect of schooling on students in the Caribbean, particularly girls. The three theories she identifies as liberal, socialist and radical.

Liberal feminists operate with the basic assumption that social systems are essentially unjust, and sexual inequalities result from factors such as prejudice, traditional values and lack of proper role models. Socialist feminist educators offer an alternative perspective and insist that any explanation of social and sexual inequality has to take account of the interconnection between ideological and economic forces in which patriarchy and capitalism reinforce each other. Socialist feminists take their cue from Marxist educators who claim that schooling, through a variety of covert and overt methods, reproduces the capitalist system. Radical feminism is concerned with two main perspectives: first, that patriarchy is of overarching importance, and second, that the personal is political. Their research focus has been on the patriarchal processes of schooling and power relations between the genders as well as the role played by sexuality in the oppression of girls in the classroom and women in the staff room.

The concerns articulated by Geofroy (2007) and Bailey (1998) are similar to those identified by other studies cited earlier in this work, such as Conley and Goldman (1994), which contain a critique of how power is exercised. Bailey's assertion that the views of postmodernist and poststructuralist feminists on educational research are emergent appear to remain true. Geofroy, in his discourse on the urgent nature of the need for redescription of the Caribbean male, expresses the view that in the Caribbean much of hegemonic hyper-masculine images seem to emanate from Jamaica, and cites Odette Parry (2000), who found that respondents in a survey from Barbados and St Vincent identified Jamaica as the "home" or "leader" of the "macho West Indian male" image and spoke about how adolescent males were increasingly influenced by the music and dancehall scene emanating from Jamaica.

Yet another Caribbean scholar whose work represents an attempt to connect postmodernism to education is Miller (1989). In a controversial paper entitled "Gender Composition of the Primary School Teaching Force: A Result of Personal Choice?", Miller (1989), in going beyond the liberal feminist sex-role socialization paradigm (which traditionally is used to explain numerical differences in the participation of the genders in the teaching force), draws on postmodernist ideology in moving away from the "universals" of earlier feminisms and argues from the perspective of plurality and diversity.

The prisms of plurality and diversity are postmodern in character and are arguably premises of Miller's theory of "place". This theory of "place" postulates that society is organized and structured on the basis of multiple criteria. These criteria determine the *place* of individuals in society in terms of their centrality or marginality. Miller's theory can be further interpreted as affirming that determinants of place include time (location in history) and space (geographical location) as well as gender and race. This theory of place reflects a postmodern epistemology, as inherent in the theory is the question, "How can *one* know the place of an individual in society?" More specifically, the research that informed Miller's paper sought answers to the question: "What explains the composition of gender in the primary school teaching force?" The answer given by Miller's research was that a sex-role paradigm was not the sole factor, as was accepted for centuries, but that a variety (plurality) of factors was responsible such as place of origin, family connections, social standing and education, among others.

Still, there are people who question the relevance of postmodernism to the Caribbean, arguing that postmodernism is just another western European, Anglo-Saxon, capitalist notion that bears no relation to the reality of poor countries that are trying to cope with basic "bread and butter" issues. Ramphal (1997) disagrees that the notion of postmodernism is of no relevance to the Caribbean and argues that several important developments outside and within the English-speaking Caribbean over the past decade now make this theory and its associated practice urgent for the region. Ramphal suggests that there is need for radical development theory to be laid out for a new (postmodern) generation of Caribbean radical development theorists.

I share Ramphal's sense of urgency and take account the fact that the world is governed by a geo-political and international economic system that divides the globe into trading blocks. The merchandise traded are not only material products, but ideas, philosophies, methodologies, cultural practices and political ideologies. While the Caribbean does not represent a large market area for the trading intents of the powerful countries, and while there now exists only one superpower, control of the Caribbean remains critical to the foundations of America's and western Europe's foreign policies and hegemonic ambitions. The same applies to Africa, Asia and the Pacific, though China, now a major player in global politics, should be factored into future analyses. Thus, to the extent that postmodernism has become an intellectual, political, epistemological and cultural reality for Europe and North America it will be for the rest of the world. My assertion, therefore, that the phenomenon is relevant is not simply an admission of the inevitable: it is a call to define a framework for deeper analysis.

Second, unlike Africa, Asia and the Pacific, the Caribbean lies in close proximity to North America and the frontiers of western Europe. As a consequence, the issues of influence and control become more critical and thus the further justification for the development of an analytic frame of reference. Thirdly, with the advent of the information "superhighway" cultures around the globe and certainly in the Caribbean have instant access to what is taking place around the world. In addition, the cultural practices and behaviours of youths around the world, in school and out of school, bear striking similarities. In some cases, the behaviours, tastes and expectations are identical. Students, like customers of modern businesses, are more informed and more demanding. The striking similarities are possible because of the penetrating influence of cable networks such as Black Entertainment Television and marketing strategies of companies such as Nike, Nokia, Google and Facebook. The behaviours of teens on the streets of downtown Cincinnati (Ohio), New York City, Trincity (Trinidad), Kingston (Jamaica) and Lyons (France) are hardly differentiable. Such is the influence of modern means of communication and therein lies the impact of postmodernism on the world which may be described as a social media village.

Postmodernism: The New Dynamics of Power in an Era of Social Media

Perhaps the most noticeable manifestation of postmodernism is social media. It is the space in which ideas are most actively traded today and the most influential leaders are those who have acquired the skill of manipulating social media. Postmodernism is, at its heart, the evidence of a borderless world where power no longer resides with a few who control wealth but with those who can persuade others to their way of thinking, believing and behaving with a tweet or some other form of communication.

Trading in ideas is what leadership is about. Management is about force, executive authority, the power to compel and force compliance. Leadership is about influence, inspiration and motivation. Whereas executive authority is the currency of management, influence is ultimately the currency of leadership. Whether leadership is being exercised in the church, the community-based organization, a company or a country, it is the capacity to influence that will set a successful leader apart from their less successful peers. Today, the tool that is most effective in trading the wares of influence is social media. Social media represents a levelling of the leadership landscape as anyone can take to social media and create a following that can be decisive in shaping public opinions, including which party to elect in a general election.

But social media is more than a weapon in the hands of the politician running for office who may consider that their success will be a function of how well the "weapon" is used. More fundamentally, social media is a tool in the hands of the electorate. With social media, the electorate can hold elected officials to account more strictly, more quickly and more effectively. The electorate can indeed use social media to "wage war" on elected officials, and therein lies the fulfilment of what may be truly called a postmodern construction of power as we behold a levelling of the traditional structures of power. Postmodernism indeed marks a new era in how power is diffused and distributed, and social media is perhaps the most potent tool for seeking the power to influence others.

The revolution brought about by social media is consistent with what Keunzli-Monard and Keunzli (2004) envisaged. They argue that postmodernism is a new era which is characterized, among other things, by the commoditization of knowledge. They suggest that other features of this new era would be contemporary management principles (participatory decision making), organizational structures (flat versus long) and research, which is now embracing qualitative methodologies and seeing them as co-equals with quantitative/positivist approaches. The essence of what Keunzli-Monard and Keunzli (2004) envisage was that there would be new modes of accessing power. Social media represents a most effective means to that end.

In relation to the issue of research methodologies, it is worth noting that while qualitative research continues to "struggle" for full acceptance in the face of continued cynicism from "quantitative/positivist" purists, significant advances have been made in establishing the parity and legitimacy of qualitative approaches. These long-in-coming advances are attributable in part to the pioneering work of people such as James, who sought to place experience at the centre of analysis. James was himself influenced by Locke (1632–1704) and Hume (1711–76) who championed the view that all human knowledge arises from sensation and experience, not innate concepts. What social media represents is a validation of personal sense; it affirms the authenticity of the subjective and the power of the subjective to become the defining perspective.

The era of postmodernism would have been preceded by at least four major periods of cultural influences that defined organizational leadership practice, which by extension had implications for educational leadership. An examination of the dominant thinking in organizational theory during those periods, and their implications for educational leadership, is undertaken in the following chapter.

3 | Leadership Approaches and Theories in Historical Perspective

Four eras of the history of modern Western civilization have been identified for the purposes of this discussion. In defining these eras, I have used the prism of management theory. In arriving at the four eras discussed below, I took into consideration the dominant theories of leadership and management and sought to classify them based on their common features. There are other classifications that could be used. The periods to which some theorists are "assigned" differ from those used by other thinkers. For example, one school of thought holds that the human relations era spans the period 1929–51. In the scheme I have used, I present the human relations era as *post–world war* and present the views of theorists beyond 1951. Thus, it is again worth emphasizing that the time periods are not hard and fast as human history does not have neatly compartmentalized eras.

Leadership styles and practices over the last one hundred years may be classified into four broad periods or eras, namely, *scientific management, human relations, behavioural science* and *post-behavioural science*.

Postmodernism has emerged at a time roughly equivalent to the last period but has extended beyond it. Postmodernism therefore represents somewhat of a fifth period. In seeking to place postmodernism in its historical context, therefore, it is necessary to explore the content of the literature on the four previous periods.

The Scientific Management Era

In the early 1900s Frederick Taylor, in advancing what has come to be known as scientific management, placed emphasis (in defining what he considered to be the proper role of leadership) on achieving efficiency and low cost of production per unit. He was indifferent, if not hostile, to notions of worker satisfaction and worker-involvement in decision making that were to emerge in the human relations era. Taylor believed that workers were lazy and used every attempt to avoid work. His approach to management was predicated on that belief.

Perhaps the chief legacy of the scientific management era is its focus on quantitative outcomes as the measures of leadership success. The thinking of the scientific managers (or classicalists, as they are sometimes called) is typical of premodern and modern modes of thought which subscribed to the notions of "grand theories". Taylor went as far as arguing that organizational success, which is the goal of management, was assured if the principles he propounded were observed. These principles included: finding the *one best way* to get the job done, selecting the *right people* to do the job and training people in the *exact* processes of production. Concepts such as *one best way, right people* and *exact* reflect a level of intolerance towards alternative ideas and approaches. This intolerance was consistent with the mode of certainty and absolutism that were features of modernist thinking. Some twenty-five to thirty-five years after Taylor's scientific management theory was advanced, the administrative management theory of Fayol, Gulick and Urwick and Weber was unveiled.

Fayol (1949), who considered himself a successful manager, having worked for several years as managing director of one of the largest coal-mining firms in France, attributed his success as a manager purely to the principles of management he used. Fayol contended that, given his success, if others followed his model they were assured of success and, like Taylor (1911) before Fayol (1949), he believed that if these activities were carefully executed consistent with the principles of scientific management, the organization must be successful. This is another example of the belief that one "grand theory" was applicable to all situations; a perspective that postmodernism critiques in its call for diversity, the embrace of mini-narratives and the acceptance of the idea of multiple truths.

The ideas of Gulick and Urwick (1937) were in line with that of Fayol (1949). They coined the acronym POSDCoRB which identified seven functions of management – *planning, organizing, staffing, directing, coordinating, reporting* and *budgeting*. These activities Gulick and Urwick described as the main functions of administration. They too hold that provided these activities were carried out with due process and care the leadership of the organization was doing what it was required to do. While these functions are undoubtedly critical to the work of any complex organization, the tacit claim that they encapsulate all the important tasks of management and leadership is again reflective of the absolutism of *modernist* thinking.

Weber (1947) contributed to the debate on the nature of administration in his *Theory of Social and Economic Organization*. This work is considered to be a seminal piece on the concept of bureaucracy. This concept of bureaucracy is based on the notions of rationality and impersonal operations. Weber (1947), like Gulick and Urwick (1937) held views which are similar to those of Fayol (1949). He argued that bureaucratic organizations were goal-oriented and rational. Bureaucratic organizations have clearly stated and published goals, determined by the hierarchy who direct their accomplishments. Bureaucratic organizations have formal chains of command between different levels. The policies in bureaucratic organizations, their rules and purposes are clearly defined to guide behaviour; divisions of labour are clear, and jobs are understood, Weber asserts, and rules ensure a certain degree of uniformity of operation.

Weber (1947), like the other theorists before him, believed in the efficiency of his model, which he regarded as indispensable to organizational success. In his view, the worth of a manager was to be measured relative to how well he understood and worked with bureaucracy. It was this rigidly task-driven approach to management that produced in large measure the disquiet and discontent of the 1930s to the 1950s and which gave rise to what came to be known as the human relations approach. (Globally, the 1930s to the 1950s was a period characterized by events such as the Great Depression, World War II and the Rights Movements.)

Approaches to Educational Leadership in Scientific Management Thinking

The primary prism through which practitioners of, or believers in, scientific management see others is through the eyes of experts. Scientific managers consider themselves to know all, to know best and to be competent to get the job done. The duty of subordinates, in the view of scientific managers, is that they follow instructions and execute their functions as directed. In this thinking, leadership is not a shared or distributed responsibility but a controlled and exclusive privilege.

Educational leaders who hold the view that they know best and that the duty of subordinates is to follow instructions will typically set policies and inform others or make other decisions that affect the direction of the organization and instruct conformity and compliance. But this approach to leadership generally, and educational leadership in the Caribbean, is unlikely to be successful in a postmodern era because access to knowledge has been increased and members of educational communities have greater exposure to, and training in, leadership in alternative contexts. Thus, there is the expectation of consultation and confidence on the part of subordinates that they can make a positive contribution to the affairs of the educational enterprise, whether at the macro or micro level.

The Human Relations Era

It is perhaps ironic, but in another sense inevitable, that the "successor" theory to that of the scientific management theory should have emerged from the "ruins" of World War II. The theorists whose works came to dominate the landscape of organizational theory were known as "human relations theorists".

A number of theorists have attracted the label "human relations theorists" (some of whom began their work before World War II). Among them are Mayo (1933), Barnard (1938), McGregor (1960) and Herzberg (1966), and human relations theorists believed that the building of harmonious relationships in the work place was fundamental to productivity and therefore ought to be the mantra of leaders. In the absence of harmony there would be low productivity. The *human relations approach* is considered to have started with a series of studies conducted at the Hawthorne Plant of Western Electric by Elton Mayo and his associates. The Hawthorne studies have strongly influenced administrative theory.

Mayo (1933) and his associates found, however, that friendships and other personality variables were more important in achieving productivity than were physical conditions. It was based on these experiments that human relations theorists were able to show the sophistication and influence of the informal organization.

Among the conclusions that Mayo (1933) made was that the informal organization was the arena in which many worker attitudes, which could determine the success of leaders, were shaped. One of the theories of leadership that emerged from these findings was that the success of a leader was dependent on how well they could "use" the informal organization while operating in the formal organization.

Barnard (1938) looked at leadership in cooperative systems. In his book *The Functions of the Executive,* he details the lack of attention to the informal organization. He stressed that informal groups can be used effectively in planning and organizing. The leader should find who the leaders are and get them to effect desired changes. He argues that the manager should attend to the needs and aspirations of the individual on the one hand and the needs and purposes of the organization on the other. Barnard also acknowledges the importance of the informal organization and posits that the needs and aspirations of individuals are often communicated through the informal organization.

Barnard's main thesis is the maintenance of morale, which he contends is significantly related to production. He argues that the main business of a leader is the maintenance of morale. The first signs of declining worker morale are often seen through the informal organization he contends. He believed and taught that the main business of the executive is the maintenance of heightened morale as the assurance of production. This task required that the leader should stay "close" to the informal organization. He concludes that if people are satisfied and happy, they will produce.

Manley (1975), whose major contribution to the development of modern Jamaica and the non-aligned movement was that of defining the place of the worker as an equal stakeholder in the affairs of the corporation, argues in *A Voice of the Workplace* that workers have a desire, and a right, to be involved in the making of decisions that affect their lives. Thus, the Manley regime of the 1970s passed a host of legislation giving the worker the right of participation and ownership in state-run companies and promoted that model to private companies.

Maslow (1970) argued, among other things, that workers needed to socialize and identify with others to satisfy the needs for esteem, sense of achievement and their level of satisfaction, contended that when this happens the worker will be motivated to achieve more in the organization. Needs theorists also stress that democracy and participation in decision making are necessary ingredients in inspirational or, what has come to be known as, transformational leadership.

McGregor's (1960) Theory Y, which was first articulated as a theory of engagement, was developed in response to what he called incorrect or wrong (X) theories about employees. The proponents of these "X" theories, according to McGregor, were the scientific managers who held that workers were lazy, lacking in ambition, disliked responsibility, inherently self-centred and preferred to be led. He contended that this view of the average employee was simply wrong and posited an opposite view, which he called Theory Y.

Herzberg (1966) discusses the issue of levels of need and explains that there are two types of need stimuli – dissatisfiers and motivators. Dissatisfiers are those tasks and outcomes which are predictable, repetitive and engage the mental faculties in a limited way. Herzberg lists among dissatisfiers factors such as clean work environment, salary and monotonous work. Their presence he says is not likely to motivate, but their absence (especially salary and the normal work environment) will demotivate, whereas challenging tasks and increased responsibility are likely to motivate.

Ouchi (1981) found that Japanese managers were more likely to encourage subordinates to participate in decision making and were more welcoming of suggestions from these subordinates. Partly because of this collaboration in arriving at decisions, Japanese managers were found to be less likely to make quick, unilateral decisions. In addition, Japanese managers were found to have the tendency to show greater concern for the welfare of workers than did American managers. This participatory, collaborative, time-consuming, decision-making process Ouchi calls Theory Z.

Approaches to Educational Leadership in Human Relations Thinking

The implicit assumption of human relations theory is that it is a mistake to exclude non-executive or non-senior members of the organization from involvement in decision making. The human relations theorists essentially contend that to have operated businesses on the basis of exclusive and cloistered decision making was a bad idea as workers are not the lazy and incompetent people that they are often made out to be. Thus, the call is for leaders to show greater faith in the capacities and commitment of workers, give them the benefit of the doubt and open the doors to the places of decision making and allow for participation.

The limitation of this thinking in the educational context in the Caribbean is that practitioners do not regard the opening of the spaces for participation in decision making as an act of generosity or graciousness. In as much as students, in the survey, expressed the expectation that their teachers and principals would consult them, it is reasonable to extrapolate that other stakeholders, such as teachers, expect to be included in decision making as a matter of good practice and even common sense. The fact that students, in the survey, held that effective leadership involved responsiveness to criticism, for example, is evidence that there is the view within the educational community that those who make decisions do not always know best and that the decisions made by those who have the power to do are not always the best decisions. Thus, the principle of participatory decision making is not to be based on pity, as this is inconsistent with how the postmodern practitioner wishes to gain access; rather, participatory decision making is to be based on the principle that others have the capacity to advance and enrich the agenda of the organization.

The Behavioural Science Era

Taking its cue from the research of Pavlov and Skinner, whose work in the early twentieth century laid the basic foundations for applying the principle of causality in human behaviour, behavioural scientists have come to view leadership styles as a variable in determining the behaviour of members of the organization as well as organizational performance.

A number of scholars have found that a relationship exists between the behaviour of the leader and that of members of the organization. These include Batista-Taran et al. (2009), who explored the role of leadership style in employee engagement; Hamidifar (2010), who studied the relationship between leadership style and employee job satisfaction; Almansour (2012), who examined the relationship between leadership style and the motivation of managers; Pradeep and Prabhu (2011) and Shafie, Baghersalimi, and Barghi (2013), who found that there was a relationship between leadership style and employee performance.

Thus, the view that leadership styles should be treated as critical, independent variables when measuring organizational success while having been the subject of much debate and controversy in the late twentieth century is emerging towards being a settled issue. The debate has spawned such territory as the differences between autocratic and democratic styles; the characteristics of transactional versus transformational leadership; people-centred versus product-centred leadership; and paradigm-paralysed versus paradigm-pioneering leadership and with a number of studies drilling down on more narrow variables, as the sampling of works above indicates.

Likert (1987), whose work was first published in 1967, was among the first thinkers to link organizational success to the internal characteristics of the organization. He posited that the success of an organization was determined by chain links of causes and effects. One of the posited causal links consists of causal variables which are factors controlled by the administration, according the Likert. These factors represent choices that the management of the organization makes which include the organization's structure, the leadership's operating philosophies, modalities of decision-making and problem-solving approaches. The choices that the management makes in relation to structure, style, operating philosophy, strategies, systems and the character of relationships are major determinants of the management culture of the organization as well as the *interaction-influence* system that dominate the organization's culture, Likert argues.

The views of Likert were based on research designed to examine the effect of management systems on employees' attitudes and behaviour and are captured in a model that identifies four management systems which characterized organizational climates. These systems he labelled Systems 1, 2, 3 and 4 (see table 3.1). These systems are essentially modes of thought and behaviour that are deemed to be characteristic of leaders and managers. According to Likert, System 1 represents the negative end of a continuum while System 4 was positive. For example, in decision-making processes, System 1 is characterized by lack of confidence in subordinates; System 2 shows a condescending level of

Table 3.1. Leadership Grid[a] Concern for People

9/1,9: Country club management									9,9: Team management
8									
7									
6									
5				5,5: Middle of the road management					
4									
3									
2									
1/1,1: Impoverished management									9,1: Authority compliance management
1	2	3	4	5		6	7	8	9

[a] The Managerial Grid developed by Robert R. Blake and Jane Mouton, republished as the Leadership Grid by Robert R. Blake and Anne Adams McCanse.

trust and confidence; System 3 has substantial but not complete confidence and trust and still wishes to keep control of decisions; and System 4 is characterized by complete confidence and trust in subordinates to make responsible and wise decisions. System 4 was deemed to be the most favourable for producing high performance as subordinates feel free to discuss ideas about their job with their supervisors, who always try to make constructive use of them. Likert further notes that System 4 interactions create intervening variables that in turn influence the nature of communication and other critical aspects of organizational functioning. The performance of the organization, he concludes, which is measured in its *end-result* variables, depends heavily on the internal functioning of the organization. This internal functioning relates principally to the supervisor–supervisee interaction.

Blake and Mouton (1994) developed the leadership grid in which they sought to help managers identify their leadership styles. The grid has two axes – Concern for People and Concern for Production – and was intended to demonstrate the bi-dimensional nature of leadership. As shown in table 3.1 the gird identifies a range of management behaviours based on the characteristics described on the two axes.

Style 1,1 at the lower left-hand corner of the grid represents low concern for people and low concern for production. This style of leadership is sometimes referred to as laissez-faire management. Style 1,9 (top left) is characterized by high concern for employees but low concern for production. The diametrical opposite to 1,9 is 9,1 leadership style (task or authoritarian management), which shows high concern for production and efficiency but low concern for employees.

Style 5,5 is middle-of-the-road management, which represents an intermediate amount of concern for both production and employee satisfaction. Style 9,9 is called team or democratic leadership and is based on an approach of high concern for improved performance. Blake and Mouton insist that the performance of subordinates is dependent on the style of leadership provided. The views of Blake and Mouton (1994) are shared by a number of thinkers, including Hersey and Blanchard (1982).

The preferred style (9,9), according to Blake and Mouton (1994), is consistent with what the postmodernist educator Beck (1993) calls "leadership of engagement". This style allows for the imagination and creativity of many other stakeholders to flourish.

The curiosity about "leadership of engagement" (the extent of dialogical and democratic processes in the school system) arises from a prior interest in whether the principles and paradigms of a postmodern era have affected the secondary school system. The postmodern spirit has affected other organizations and has forced a shift in relationships between the different sectors and layers of these organizations. The school is an open system (organization) that is fed by inputs from the external environment, and as such is expected to show signs of impact from the influence of postmodernism.

Mead (1934), in articulating what has come be known as the Social Action Theory, stresses that the individual's need for involvement in the making of decisions that affect their lives is based on the fact that individuals are not only acted upon by their environments but also act upon their own environments. One implication of Mead's position is that in order for students to meaningfully interact with their environment, they will need training in the processes of meaningful interaction. This training is likely to occur in an environment that facilitates their impacting their environment – sharing mini-narratives.

This "counter-action" friendly environment in schools relates both to administrative as well as pedagogical leadership. This acting upon one's environment is what Berger and Luckmann (1967) calls a social (re-)construction of reality. This notion of acting on one's reality is consistent with the postmodern reality that social truths and power relations are variations on themes that are subjective. The process of de-construction is not only concerned therefore with *"What is true?"* but *"Whose truth?"*, postmodernists contend. As Beck posits, purposes and contexts vary from individual to individual and from group to group, what therefore one asserts as true is something of a personal narrative, an arrival at one's own particular "site" in the world.

The behavioural science era is focused on certain kinds of organizational relationships. Hallinger and Heck (1996) examined the empirical literature that emerged during the fifteen-year period from 1980 to 1995, which looks at the effects of the principals' leadership. From their review of over forty studies, they identified various models used to investigate the relationship between school leadership and student achievement. They identified three models which were labelled "direct effect", "mediated effect" and "reciprocal effect".

The "direct-effect" model suggests that leaders' practices can have effects on school outcomes and that these can be measured apart from other related variables. The "mediated-effect" model hypothesizes that leaders achieve their effect on school outcomes through indirect paths. That is, other people, events and organizational and cultural factors mediate the leaders' contribution. With respect to the "reciprocal-effect" model, Hallinger and Heck suggest that relationships between the principal and features of the school and its environment were interactive. This model implies that school leaders adapt to the organization in which they work, changing their thinking and behaviour over time. Thus, the adaptation of thinking with the passage of time, relative to leadership styles, will inevitably be a product of reciprocity.

Approaches to Educational Leadership from a Behavioural Science Perspective

A behavioural science perspective on leadership suggests that certain types of organizational systems and structures, such as bureaucracies, are inherently opposed to the principles and processes of shared leadership and shared learning. Bureaucratic organizations are by design deemed to be inconsistent with the qualities of autonomy, freedom to doubt, space to debate, the expectation of consultation and the beauty of diversity and difference, which are characteristics of a postmodern era. Thus, while there must be structured processes for auditable and accountable decision-making processes in educational leadership practices, the emphasis on bureaucracy as the primary method of engagement risks isolating the creativity and innovative bent of emerging leaders and differentiated learners whose postmodern spirits are more patient with experiment and change. In this change-patient era, emerging leaders and learners desire greater autonomy over their actions and are thus less comfortable with the strictures of bureaucracy and authoritarianism. Thus, the postmodern classroom, like the postmodern boardroom, calls for greater freedom to share ideas, working in circular structures (as against working in hierarchies) and producing results collaboratively (as against producing individualized outputs).

The Post-Behavioural Science Era

Murphy (1990) argues that the next era in the development of the educational administration is the post-behavioural science era. Among the issues on which leaders will be expected to focus during this era are issues such as justice, community and inclusiveness (democracy). The post-behavioural science era is a by-product of postmodernism. This school of thought emphasizes democracy and social justice issues, positing what has been labelled emergent non-traditional perspectives. The emphasis on democracy is consistent with the findings of Gordon and Reese (1997), who found that teachers were increasingly being alienated from the school's processes because of undemocratic approaches to curriculum and instruction, resulting from indirect control. This indirect control, which represented a different type of accountability, was limiting the influence of leadership in a school setting. They found that there was lowering faculty morale and negative effects on school-community relations.

What Murphy (1990) articulates is a new paradigm of leadership and an approach to understanding organizational climates. Without a doubt, social justice issues are among the major focuses of the current era. Issues that were once viewed in moralistic terms are now viewed as issues of "rights". Thus, participation in decision making, sharing power and relaxing the strictures of bureaucracy are no longer seen as nice things to do, or, worse, as reflections of graciousness; they are now seen as issues of rights.

The post-behavioural science era is, however, not simply about the issues of "rights". Speaking on the issue of the need to be sensitive to the type of era in which schools now operate, Foster (2004) advocates the development of "local" leadership. In the context of his research "local" was used in contradistinction to regional and state. He lamented the fact that the school's role in developing a democratic polity was being eroded by the existence of excessive rules and regulations, political interference and whimsical and impulsive decisions by people who have had very limited exposure to the realities that confront people in their contexts. Foster, therefore, emphasized the need for the local school community to have a larger and more significant involvement in its operations.

Foster (2004) sees the notion of community resulting in restructured classrooms and redefined administration (read "democracy"), among other things. It is the contention of this researcher that the metaphor of community has implications for the attitudes students have towards individual differences and therefore alternative approaches and points of view. Thus, schools which function as communities will be more tolerant of, and patient with, strategies which are not necessarily born of the leader or are not necessarily to their liking, and in cases where strategies not born of the leader fail to produce the expected outcomes, the emphasis will be on learning lessons from the experience rather than assigning blame.

Approaches to Educational Leadership in a Post-Behavioural Science Era

A post-behavioural science era speaks to the democratizing of education and involves giving students greater control over their learning (Beck 1993). In the same way that control over the processes and outcomes is loosened in relation to students, a similar loosening is expected in relation to other participants such as teachers in relation to the powers of principals, and teachers, principals and school boards in relation to the powers of education officers and ministry officials. Beck (1993) further states that teachers should encourage students to dialogue with them and other theorists rather than "drinking in", in an uncritical way, what teachers and theorists say. The same principle should be applicable at all levels of the hierarchy. At all levels of the educational system there should be encouragement to interrogate: interrogate ideas, decisions, policy prescriptions, strategies and programmes. This interrogation should be driven by an attempt to find better and more contextually relevant ways of solving the problems that are peculiar to each context. This is not to suggest, as Beck (1993) concedes, that there is no room for some measure of expertise, the distinctions between "expert" and "non-expert" have been blurred or removed in post-behavioural science era.

A post-behavioural science era has morphed into a postmodern era and the characteristics between the two are not significant. The two are sometime imperceptible and their effects similar. A new paradigm of post-behavioural science and postmodernism (but more so the latter), is Proposition MRM. Proposition MRM is an emergent theory of leadership that seeks to define a framework for educational practice at both the policy determination and practitioner level. The dimensions of Proposition MRM are explored in this chapter, whereas the relationship between Proposition MRM and educational leadership in the Caribbean discussed in chapter 4, and the nature of educational leadership in a postmodern era examined in chapter 5. Chapter 6 provides reflections on overall arguments of this book and their relevance to educational leadership. These reflections are offered by a policymaker and former educational practitioner as well as a current practitioner.

4 | Proposition MRM

The insights for Proposition MRM were derived from a study conducted between 2004 and 2008, designed to understand the perceptions and expectations that students have of leaders, in a postmodern era. The research was driven by two main questions, namely:

1. What are the perceptions and expectations that students have of the leadership of their teachers and principals and are these perceptions and expectations tenets of postmodernism?
2. What are the comparisons between the perceptions and expectations of students and what the scientific literature says about people's expectations of leaders in a postmodern era?

Given the context within which the research was done and having regard to other literature, discussed below, I have come to the view that the answer to these questions provides a perspective on the parameters within which we must examine the nature of educational leadership in the Caribbean.

The study found three factors which accounted for 61.855 per cent of the variation in the data. These factors were modelling, respect and motivation (MRM). Figure 4.1 shows the scree plot and the position of the variables to each other.

Figure 4.2 shows the weighting of the top three variables. The first variable is modelling which accounts for 34.161 per cent of the variation in the data as can be seen in second to last column in figure 4.2. The second variable refers to

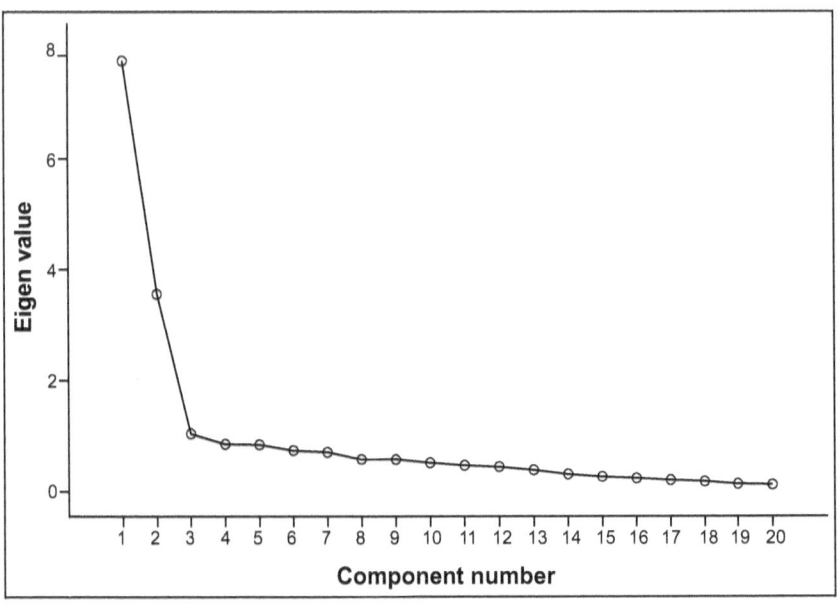

Figure 4.1. Scree plot showing top three factors.

Total Variance Explained

Component	Initial Eigenvalues			Extraction Sums of Squared Loadings			Rotation Sums of Squared Loadings		
	Total	% of Variance	Cumulative %	Total	% of Variance	Cumulative %	Total	% of Variance	Cumulative
1	7.760	38.798	38.798	7.760	38.798	38.798	6.832	34.161	34.1
2	3.563	17.815	56.613	3.563	17.815	56.613	4.298	21.489	55.6
3	1.048	5.242	61.855	1.048	5.242	61.855	1.241	6.204	61.8
4	.859	4.297	66.152						
5	.850	4.252	70.404						
6	.745	3.727	74.130						
7	.713	3.567	77.697						
8	.584	2.920	80.617						
9	.581	2.904	83.521						
10	.518	2.592	86.113						
11	.473	2.364	88.476						
12	.446	2.228	90.704						
13	.387	1.934	92.638						
14	.311	1.555	94.193						
15	.268	1.338	95.532						
16	.241	1.206	96.738						
17	.207	1.036	97.774						
18	.183	.914	98.688						
19	.138	.691	99.379						
20	.124	.621	100.000						

Extraction Method: Principal Component Analysis.

Figure 4.2. Percentage distribution of variation factors.

	Component		
	1	2	3
Principal as role model	.880	.181	.102
Principal as leader	.868	.178	.099
Principal's respect for students	.868	.109	.045
Principal's interest in students' concerns	.862	.119	.135
Students' respect for principal	.848	.034	.020
Principal as listener	.836	.226	.057
Principal's sharing of decision making	.821	.113	.066
Principal's attitude to underperformers	.778	.041	.139
Comfort with expressing disagreement	.681	.002	.144
Principal's encouragement of critical thinking	.650	.070	-.042
Feeling of being respected by teacher	.133	.769	.026
Teacher as listener	.021	.750	.110
Teacher acceptance of correction	.225	.715	-.055
Relationship with teacher	.158	.694	.178
Teacher as role model	.107	.667	.234
Teacher encouragement of self-confidence	.074	.641	.369
Respect for teacher	.155	.614	.019
Teacher interest in students' opinions	-.087	.579	.248
Teacher excitement in teaching	.178	.434	.305
Level of motivation	.178	.167	.728
Preparation for life	.041	.154	.702
Student attitude to others	.185	.172	.687
Impact of teaching style on motivation	-.092	.476	.490

Extraction Method: Principal Component Analysis.
Rotation Method: Varimax with Kaiser Normalization.
^aRotation converged in 5 iterations.

Figure 4.3. Rotated component matrix.^a

respect and this accounts for 21.489 per cent of the variation in the data. The final of the top three variables is motivation which accounts for 6.204 per cent of the variation in the data.

The top three factors mentioned above, and their constituent elements are detailed in figure 4.3 identified as the rotated component matrix. The three variables, MRM, are identified as explained below.

In the first column of figure 4.3 are the words, "principal as role model" as beside those words in the second column is the weighting of that variable stated as .880. It is from that wording that the first variable "model" is derived, which represents the M in Proposition MRM. All the items listed under the "principal as model" down to "principal's encouragement of critical thinking", which has a weighting of .650, are elements of being a model. Below the weighting .650 is the number .133 which is appears to correspond to the words, "feeling of being respected by teacher". These words signal the second variable "respect", the R in Proposition MRM for which the actual weighting is shown in the second column at .769. The fact that this number, .769 is greater than .650 above is the indication that it is a separate variable and is distinct from modelling. All the items under "feeling of being respected by teacher" down to "teacher excitement in teaching" and elements of the variable "respect". The weighting for "teacher excitement in teaching" is .434 across from which is a lower number of .305. This indicates that "teacher excitement in teaching" is the last item under the variable respect. Below the .305 is the number .728, which corresponds to the item, "level of motivation". The .728, which is larger than .434, signals that another variable has emerged. This third variable is "motivation", which is represented by the second M in Proposition MRM.

The factors were generated using the software programme Statistical Packages for the Social Sciences. The instrument that was used to gather the data is in the appendix section.

The data in figure 4.3 are represented in table 4.1.

The constituent elements of Proposition MRM as shown in table 4.1 show the relationship between the top three factors and the related sub-factors. It is my

Table 4.1. Factors of Proposition MRM

1	2	3
Role Model	**Respect**	**Motivation**
Principal as leader	Teacher as listener	Preparation for life
Principal's respect for students	Relationship with teacher	Student attitudes to others
Principal's interest in students' concerns	Teacher acceptance of correction	Impact of teaching style on motivation
Students' respect for principal	Teacher as role model	
Principal as listener	Teacher encouragement of self-confidence	
Principal's sharing of decision making	Respect for teacher	
Principal's attitude to underperformers	Teacher's interest in student's opinions	
Comfort with expressing disagreement with principal	Teacher excitement in teaching	
Principal's encouragement of critical thinking		

reliance on these findings and taking account of other perspectives in the scientific literature, I have come to the conclusion that MRM are among the critical qualities that should inform the practice of, and approach to, educational leadership in the Caribbean. This assertion I have called *Proposition MRM*.

The exploration of Proposition MRM is aided by the application of three interrogatives, namely:

1. **What** is the chief quality by which a transformational leader is known? The answer, as disclosed by the research, is that the chief characteristic of the transformational leader is that they *model* the qualities and behaviours to which they call others to display. In this regard, the underlying assumption is that the task of transformation is a shared one and thus, by modelling the behaviours expected of others, the leader is setting the tone for everyone to be active contributors to the process of transforming the organization or community. In essence the leader shows, not merely says, what transformational leadership behaviours are, and in the process calls on members of the organization to engage in transformational conduct.
2. **How** should the leader relate? The answer given by the data is that the leader should show *respect* to those they lead (and presumably all others). The further answer, as supported by the data, is that the leader is expected to show regard for the skills and abilities, opinions, perspectives, needs and aspirations of others within the organization or community they lead. This display of respect, as the later discussion will show, includes engagement in decision making and shaping the direction of the organization or community.
3. **Where** the energies of the leader should be focused? Implicit in this question is that leaders, even though well intentioned, can misdirect their energies as well as the energies (and resources) of the organization and, should this happen the organization will live the consequences. The foregoing assumption may be expressed without the implied judgement by simply noting that the areas in which a leader focuses their energies and that of the organization or community, has consequences for good or for ill.

The answer, given by the data, to the question "Where should the energies of the leader be focused?" is that those energies should be focused on motivating others. Motivation, according to the data, involves inspiring others by engaging them to share in the vision of the organization or community, by helping them to grasp the bigger picture and by enlisting their support in the pursuit of attaining the goals of the organization. The immediate impact of this is that when a leader sets goals for the organization, they are not merely setting personal targets, nor are they able to attain those targets without support. The attainment of organizational goals depends on the commitment and support of members of the organization and the task of the leader includes providing members of the organization with the relevant information about those targets, and the inspiration for them to energetically pursue those targets.

Thus, the claim of this book is that the three factors, MRM, are major characteristics of the practice of educational leadership not only at the micro (or school level) – the context in which the data were collected – but also at all levels of, and beyond, the education system.

Proposition MRM as a Paradigm for Power Sharing

Proposition MRM challenges some existing notions of educational leadership as well as reinforces others which have sought to dispute traditional approaches to leadership and pedagogy as well as the some practices of schooling which have tended to place those in authority in positions of superiority to the rest of the community. I explore three areas in which Proposition MRM both challenge traditional assumptions as well as reinforce others.

Pearce, Wassenaar and Manz (2014) suggest that power sharing is the key to team success. This view is also held by Kocolowski (2010), who argues that, given the complexity of today's organizations, it is impossible for one individual to provide effective leadership of the organization. Thompson (2015) contends that any leader who thinks they can single-handedly transform an organization is being either naïve or dishonest.

A postmodern era is characterized as increasingly demanding a consultative and power-sharing approach. This research has shown that the secondary school system appears to be challenged to consider the implications of postmodernism for its leadership practices including decision-making processes. One of the well-known fears that some leaders have is that of being perceived as being weak if they rely heavily on consultation. A consultative and power-sharing approach does not, as conventional and fundamentalist views suggest, portray a weak, insecure and indecisive leader; rather, it reflects a confident leader who is focused on getting the best out of their team.

Ouchi (1981) found that Japanese managers were more likely to encourage subordinates to participate in decision making, and were more welcoming of suggestions from these subordinates. Largely because of this collaboration in arriving at decisions, Japanese managers were found to be less likely to make quick, unilateral decisions. The success of Japanese companies has been in part attributed to their collaborative approach to decision making. The collaborative approach is predicated on the view that the success of the enterprise is "ours", whereas insular decision-making approaches operates on the basis that success is "mine".

Fayol (1949) contended that his success as a leader of an organization was the product of reliance on clearly designed systems that he had created, the effectiveness of which was constantly evaluated in order to ensure that they were producing desired results. Weber (1947), like the other theorists before him, believed in the efficiency of his model, which he regarded as indispensable to organizational success. These models emphasized that decision making was to be the preserve of senior people only and, in effect, bracketed-out consultation and employee involvement in the process.

Mayo (1933), Barnard (1938) and Simon (1957) reflected a sensitivity to shared decision making that contrasted with the emphasis of Weber and Fayol and, along with others, pioneered what came to be known as the "human relations approach", which articulated the value of consultation and involvement. The work of the human relations "pioneers" was strengthened by McGregor (1960), whose Theory X and Theory Y redefined the worker. The case for greater employee involvement in decision making was further strengthened by a number of other scholars and researchers, chief among them Blake and Mouton (1994), Gordon and Reese (1997), Hersey and Blanchard (1982), Ouchi (1981), and Peters and Watermann (1982). While the work of these authors (listed above) focused on business organizations, there is an equally long list of scholars who have examined the democratization of schools and promulgate the need for sharing of the authority and decision making in schools. These include Hallinger (1992), Conley and Goldman (1994), Poplin (1992), Sheppard (1996), Sergiovanni (1991), and Campion, Papper and Medsker (1996), all of whom advance the view that the power of principals need to be shared in more structured and ongoing ways with teachers.

Beck (1993) postulates that the postmodern classroom must be a more dialogical and democratic learning environment than the premodern classroom in which the teacher was expert. Pescuric and Byham (1996) see leadership and teaching as actions in which the leader/teacher models appropriate behaviours for others to emulate, thereby creating a more egalitarian learning environment. Kaye and Jacobson (1996) emphasize that leading and teaching largely involve mentoring, while Cusimano (1996) sees teaching primarily as facilitation.

Although there has been considerable forward movement in the debate over the models of organizational power sharing since the time of Fayol and Weber, and while many business and tertiary educational institutions have embraced the notion of power sharing to include stakeholders at the lowest levels of the power hierarchy, notions of power sharing at the level of secondary schooling have not shown an inclination to include students in power sharing to a degree comparable to what obtains in businesses that have adopted approaches driven by total quality. Under TQM, the most junior level of workers are given the opportunity to make or participate in significant decisions about the operation of their organizations. Beck seems to have gone the farthest in articulating a power-sharing paradigm involving students, but his focus is on the classroom situation.

Using the prism of postmodernism which, among other things, posits that the current social milieu in which schools operate has increased the desire of stakeholders for greater consultation and involvement in decision making, and relying on the authority of Erickson, Vygotsky and Beck, I sought to examine the extent to which students perceived that they were (or ought to be) consulted in the decision-making process of their schools. The result of a cross tabulation on the variable, "my principal takes the views of students into consideration before making some decisions", showed that two-thirds of males of the 67 males who responded were either unsure or disagreed, with the percentage of those disagreeing or strongly disagreeing accounting for 43 per cent. By contrast, only a third of the 84 females were either unsure or disagreed with the definitive positions (disagree/strongly disagree), accounting for a mere 7 per cent.

The finding that 43 per cent of males feel that the principal does not take students' views into consideration before making some decisions compared to a mere 7 per cent of females has two possible interpretations. The first probable explanation is that males have a greater desire for involvement and the second that while they may have a greater desire for involvement they feel less involved than females do.

Fayol felt that his success as a leader of an organization was the product of reliance on clearly designed systems that he had created, the effectiveness of which was constantly evaluated in order to ensure that they were producing desired results, and about the same time Weber argued that his bureaucratic model was indispensable to organizational success. The dawn of the human relations approach, which Mayo (1933) and others facilitated, led to a new perspective on the worker. The work of these human relations theorists has focused on business organizations and a number of scholars, operating with a similar *pro-sharing of power* orientation has examined the democratization of schools, with the focus of principals sharing more power with teachers.

The expectations of students that they be involved in decision making are arguably related to their notions of the role of critical thinking in the leadership and learning contexts to which they are exposed. Critical thinking may be defined as the process of assessing ones reality and developing theories and approaches that are contextual and flexible in order to make sense of that reality. Critical thinking means finding practical solutions for the problems that one's reality presents. Critical thinking, therefore, involves probing for answers and pressuring decision makers to act rationally and responsibly and demonstrate that their decisions have taken account of all relevant factors and are in the best interest of those affected.

Proposition MRM as a Model of Critical Thinking

Lai (2011) defines critical thinking as a process which involves skills of analysing arguments, making inferences using inductive or deductive reasoning, judging or evaluating, and making decisions or solving problems. These skills, she suggests, are born of dispositions such as fair-mindedness, inquisitiveness, flexibility and a propensity to seek reason, among others. Lloyd and Bahr (2010) offer a somewhat similar characterization, which is attributed to Francis Bacon. According to this Baconian rendition, critical thinking is characterized by a the willingness and patience to doubt, slowness to assert and carefulness to dispose and set in order.

The qualities of the critical thinker, as summarized above, are aligned to the notion of respect in Proposition MRM. Guided by the question that is related to respect in the proposition's framework, "How does the leader relate?", the construct of *respect* explored whether a leader is open to affirming the skills, abilities, opinions and perspectives of others as well as whether they are supportive of their needs and aspirations in ways that lead to facilitating their involvement in decision making and shaping the direction of the organization, the community and the country. But the display of respect is not only applicable to the relationship between leader and those led, as outlined in the basic construction of *respect* in Proposition MRM; it also relates to the quality of the interaction and engagement between and among peers. The willingness to affirm others' skills, abilities and opinions, to exercise patience, and being slow to assert are among the key elements of respect.

Disagreements are inevitable among thinking people. The more one is prone to think critically and the more trained one is in critical thinking, the more likely it is that one will see things differently from others. These differences of world view mean that one will see dimensions of issues that others have not seen, and therein lies the potential for disagreements. Increasing the capacities of people to express conflicting opinions while being respectful of others is one of the purposes of schooling and is fundamentally what critical thinking is about. Critical thinking may be defined as the process of assessing ones' reality and developing theories and approaches that are contextual and flexible in order to make sense of that reality. Critical thinking means finding practical solutions for the problems that one's reality presents. Critical thinking, therefore, involves probing for answers and pressuring decision makers to act rationally and responsibly and demonstrate that their decisions have taken account of all relevant factors and are in the best interest of affected individuals.

I hold the view that whether it is in the employer-employee or teacher-student relationship, disagreement (as distinct from disagreeableness) is to be encouraged as it is through encouraging disagreement that greater or better ideas are allowed to emerge and ways of solving shared problems are improved. The management innovation/slogan TQM is related to critical thinking. TQM, as a principle, affirms that every worker is responsible for ensuring quality. As such, every worker is encouraged to question decisions, constantly evaluate processes and strive to improve on previous performances, thereby being critical of all actions and outcomes. This principle of TQM is highly applicable to the teacher-student relationship and it is probable that many of the problems faced by school administrators could be more effectively resolved if there were an attempt to deliberately engage students in the solutions-finding process. This is what successful businesses have done.

It takes a confident leader – whether supervisor or teacher – to invite a disagreement. Burkus (2013) recounts the case of Alfred P. Sloan at General Motors, who at meeting in which GM's top management team was considering a weighty decision, closed the meeting by saying, "Gentlemen, I take it we are all in complete agreement on the decision here?" Burkus relayed that Sloan then waited as each member of the committee nodded in agreement. Burkus reported that Sloan said, "Then, I propose we postpone further discussion of this matter until our next meeting to give ourselves time to develop disagreement and perhaps gain some understanding of what this decision is about."

I submit that meaningful engagement in the teaching and learning process of school as well as the production and productivity goals of an organization requires that space be created for student and employee disagreement. Batista-Taran et al. (2009), in examining the construct of employee engagement, cites Harter, Schmidt and Hayes (2002), who define engagement as the experience wherein an "individual is involved in, and experiences satisfaction with, as well as enthusiasm for work".

Batista-Taran et al. build on the work of Kahn (1990), who argues that engagement describes the intimate involvement with and framework of the work experience. This intimacy creates emotional connections to others and facilitates cognitive vigilance. In drilling down on the notion and importance of power sharing, which is the essential kernel of employee engagement, using the variables *Comfort with Disagreement* and *Encouragement of Critical Thinking*, some interesting results were found.

It is to be recalled that the sample for this research were tenth and eleventh graders, who are at the stage where, according to Erickson, they are developing their own identities and opinions and characteristically, their opinions are at odds with that of those in authority. One of the challenges that people who work with teens face, therefore, is that of developing and displaying tolerance with the "contrary" ways and ideas of teens. The interest in this issue is based on the premise that consultation is one of the critical ingredients of leadership in a postmodern era and the notion of consultation assumes that other opinions will be given an opportunity to be heard. Inevitably, contrary points of view will emerge. This issue of predicating consultation on the principle that disagreements may exist and that parties should be encouraged to articulate those disagreements is a corner stone of the concept of dialogue and is at the heart of postmodernism, which promotes democracy and celebrates diversity.

Bagnall (1994), in describing the implications of postmodernism for adult education, asserts that the tenets of postmodernism are the interpretive nature of perception and the cultural contingency of belief. He concludes that postmodernist education must be contextualized, indeterminate, expressive, participative, heterodox and critical. In a previous work, he identifies four postmodern tensions affecting continuing education, namely: aggregation versus fragmentation, consistency versus flexibility, description versus evaluation and association versus immediacy. While Bagnall confines his discussion on critical thinking to adult education, the principles are also applicable to education at other levels of the education system, particularly at the high school level during that phase in which students are expected to develop their critical-thinking skills. The contrasts that Bagnall identifies also resonate with the underlying ethic of Proposition MRM. Proposition MRM promotes an ethic of collaboration and community versus fragmentation and insularity and affirms the importance of flexibility, tentativeness and openness to new ideas versus a fixity of perspective and interpretation. Proposition MRM is fundamentally descriptive rather than evaluative and judgemental and leaves space for personal and collective application of principles, insights and ideas within a context of permissiveness to diverse approaches and new ideas.

The importance of critical thinking as an element in the ethos of postmodernism and a characteristic of Proposition MRM is encouragingly reinforced by the finding that in the original study found that 60.9 per cent of students agreed or strongly agreed that their principal encouraged this approach. A deeper analysis of the data using the two related variables showed that fairly strong correlations were found to exist between the variables *my principal encourages students to be critical thinkers (encouragement of critical thinking)/my principal is a good leader* and *encouragement of critical thinking/respect for principal,* at .487 and .464, respectively.

Proposition MRM as a Framework for Collaboration

Growe (2011) suggests that collaboration is the "new normal" for schools, noting that a combination of limited resources and more complex problems, individual schools are no longer to function on their own and neither can individual leaders within those schools successfully and sustainably solve the normal problems faced, on their own. In a similar vein, Hecht (2013) asserts that "collaboration is the new competition". He argues that leaders and organizations are increasingly coming to the realization that even their best individual efforts are not enough to face the complex and interconnected problems of the twenty-first century. In light of this, leaders are putting aside self-interests and collaborating to build a new civic infrastructure to advance their shared objectives. O'Leary and Bingham (2009) define collaboration as "the process of facilitating and operating in multi-organizational arrangements to solve problems that cannot be solved or easily solved by single organizations" (p. 565). This process involves working together to achieve common goals, working across boundaries and in multi-sector and multi-actor relationships. Collaboration, they emphasize, is based on the value of reciprocity.

Proposition MRM is based on the principle of collaboration in that it emphasizes the value of leaders working with others as well as the ultimate objective of communal leadership and decision making based on the underlying principles of shared responsibility, dispersed wisdom, inclusivity and the requirements of SD.

The reality of a common space within which human life is lived dictates the need for collaboration. Collaboration is the key to sustainability of the common space; efficiency in executing tasks that, of necessity, involve others; and effectiveness in attaining important common goals. The development of collaborative and cooperative skills is one of the principal functions of the socialization of human beings whose existence occurs within a shared common space (community). Schooling is designed to reinforce qualities which collective life demands such as the willingness to change inappropriate behaviours. But collaborative skills are not only necessary in the context of socialization: they are increasingly required in the workplace of a postmodern world, which is increasingly centred around teams, as is now being practised in many organizations.

It has been found that having students working collaboratively in groups yields much more learning than the reverse. The outcomes of this approach are many, chief of which are their social skills; tolerance of each other; and in, many cases, their academic performance. Of even greater importance is the fact that their dependence on the teacher is lessened, resulting in students feeling better about themselves. These are virtues and values that survival in a postmodern era demands.

One of the requirements of schooling, therefore, given the new directions in the workplace, is that of enabling students to develop collaborative and cooperative skills. The acquisition and application of the collaborative and cooperative skills that are demanded by a new culture, requires the engagement of the energies and interests of students. This art of engaging energies and interests is what motivation involves. The ability to motivate others is one of the most fundamental requirements of any leader. This skill depends to a significant degree on emotional intelligence (EQ) as Goleman (1998) argues. EQ describes an ability, capacity or skill to perceive, assess and manage the emotions of one's self, of others and of groups, as well as to motivate ourselves and others. EQ is the capacity to understand emotional information and to reason with emotions. These competencies are either hardly known or deemphasized in many schools and classrooms as well as leadership circles, but emerging evidence is showing that the real stars in organizations are not those who are merely technically skilled but those who are able to blend technical competence with EQ, thereby enabling others to excel because of a belief in themselves. When people believe in themselves they are more prone to collaborate because they are no longer threatened by the performance and competence of others and do not regard the superior technical skills of others as reflecting poorly on them.

One of the beautiful things about EQ, unlike technical competence, is that there is really no cap on its potential. Some people will never be able do well at mathematics or physics, for example (though in many cases they would have if they had not been led to doubt themselves), but regardless of our age and stage we can learn the art of listening, we can learn to care, respect others, be tolerant with others, learn from others, work with others and understand others.

These skills are those who are increasingly in demand in a postmodern era. These skills cannot be commoditized and therefore require self-discipline and personal awareness in order for them to be acquired. One of the requirements, then, of transformational leadership is the ability of the leader to teach others the virtue of acquiring the skills of the emotionally intelligent. This the transformational leader does by demonstrating these skills in their leadership style and then showing the spectacular results in the performance, confidence and cooperation of others.

I submit that these three interrogatives represent foundational questions in defining leadership. Thus, in so far as previous discussions on transformational leadership tended to focus on traits and charisma as primary considerations, the submission that the starting point is to be found in the interrogatives *who, how, what,* represents a reshaping of the conversation.

In supporting the view that the role of the leader is being redefined, Strock and Cabrera (2010) lists what he contends are the ten principles of leadership for the twenty-first century, and places in the first position the suggestion that "everyone can lead because everyone can serve" (Greenleaf 1970/2002).

Barton, Grant and Horn (2012) summarize interviews with six global leaders and, among other things, concluded that the operating environment of leadership may be characterized as bewildering, with very few things being certain, and the dynamics more complex than any other period in history. In light of this, today's chief executive officer (CEO) require judgement and buy-in from the team, a capacity to focus on the key decisions that need to be made at a given time (as against trying to solve several problems at once), in addition to possessing the ambition for a cause greater than self. This commitment to a cause greater than self is, I suggest, the embodiment of servant leadership.

Thompson (2013) made somewhat of a similar call pointing to the need for mutual accountability where he argued that inclusionary decision making, which shows how much value the team leader places on the capacity of team members to contribute, represents, in part, the location of effective leadership in the twenty-first century.

Proposition MRM versus Other Leadership Theories

Brown and Bryant (2015), taking account of Greenleaf's (1970/2002) characterization of servant leadership as being based on the principle of "first to serve and then to lead", examine the challenges facing servant leadership as a theoretical construct. They were particularly concerned with what they describe as the lack of construct clarity and the lack of agreed upon measures, among other things. In examining the life of Abraham Lincoln against the backdrop of what servant leadership means, they concluded that humility, empathy and servant leadership are all linked together. They further suggested that in order for a leader to be effective in their leadership role, they must know the issues that plague the followers. They further posited that the perpetual fame of Abraham Lincoln was in large part attributable to his humility and his understanding of his constituents by empathizing with them.

Zhang, Lin and Foo (2012), in a study of leadership practices in Singaporean schools, found that servant leadership was a more acceptable form of leadership than authoritative leadership. They also found that servant leadership is more effective because it reflects a better use of leaders' power. This use of the leader's power involves consultative decision making, power sharing, submission to the collective wisdom and an orientation of leadership as facilitating rather than directing and controlling.

Proposition MRM denotes an underlying philosophy of leadership that is aligned to contemporary concepts of leadership, particularly servant leadership. Proposition MRM's chief claim is that it embodies an interpretation of leadership that places greater emphasis on the extent to which the leader reflects (models) the kinds of behaviour expected of others, the degree to which respect is shown and how extensively the leader shares power and involves others in decision making Servant leadership marks a paradigm shift in leadership from a power-based/authority-based approach to one of empowerment

(Dambe and Moorad 2008), and according to Taylor (2007) is viewed as an extension of transformational leadership. Proposition MRM emphasizes power-sharing, inclusion, regard for others' abilities, consultative decision making and egalitarianism.

According to Kaye and Jacobson (1996), a servant–leader orientation to leadership appears to be a natural way of engaging by people who have evolved to a psychological location where ego and status matter very little – if at all. These individuals have come to realize that a self-focused mindset can stifle and eventually suffocate the motivation and commitment of others, and to the extent that leadership is about helping others to become their best, then the servant-leader relegates self to a place of minimal significance.

Proposition MRM is also aligned to Proposition CJC, which Thompson (2015) advances as the key elements of effective leadership in the twenty-first century. Proposition CJC refers to care, justice and capacity, and is built around the notion that effective leadership requires that leaders show that they *care* for those they lead. Caring leadership is expressed in a variety of ways but according to Thompson, the chief way in which leaders show care is by creating the conditions for others to be meaningfully involved in decision making. When leaders fail to facilitate others' meaningful involvement in decision making, the likely feeling of others will be that there has been some measure of injustice. Thus, showing care, through the creation of systems for employee engagement, is an issue of *justice*.

The justification for showing care is not to be found, Thompson suggests, in some notion of kindness and goodwill on the part of the leader. Rather, showing care is the related to the pragmatic consideration that employees/team members possess *capacities* that can advance the cause of the organization.

Proposition MRM purports to represent an extension and regrounding of other theories of leadership, including Theory XY as argued by McGregor (1960) and Theory Z as advanced by Ouchi (1981).

McGregor, a human relations theorist, posits that traditional notions of the worker as being lazy and prone to shirk responsibility and therefore having to be closely supervised were wrong (X), negative theories. On the contrary, he contends, the worker is inherently hard working, enjoys a challenge, is willing to assume responsibility and does not require close supervision; thus, Theory Y (meaning "yes" or "positive"). McGregor's theory, also known as a theory of motivation, posits that organizations that operate on the basis of "X" theories are likely to produce de-motivated workers with predictable negative consequences for the organization, while those that operate on the basis of Y theories are likely to experience opposite consequences.

Ouchi (1981) sought to understand what factors were responsible for the success of Japanese businesses compared to American businesses and found that

Japanese managers showed more concern for the welfare of workers, were less inclined to take hasty decisions and were more consultative. This style of leadership Ouchi (1981) defined as Theory Z to indicate that his work had advanced that of McGregor one step further. Looked at from a picturesque point of view and using the letters of the alphabet as an illustrative reference point, Ouchi (1981) seemed to have advanced the thinking on leadership to a critical *end* point – Z. My contention is that contrary to Ouchi's suggestion that we had completed the leadership alphabet; there are some important pieces that we missed. In retracing our steps to recover those pieces we may have missed, we have come upon three critical bits which I am calling MRM. My argument, therefore, is that in seeking to develop a theory of leadership in the current context in which schools operate, attention needs to be given to Proposition MRM.

In the research that informed this work, the first question I tried to answer was: *What are the perceptions and expectations that students have of the leadership of their teachers and principals and do these perceptions and expectations reflect the tenets of postmodernism?* The answer to the first part of the question is found in Proposition MRM, specifically that the perceptions and expectations of students are that their leaders should *model* behaviours expected of them, *respect* and *motivate* them. The second part of the first research question required a determination to be made as to whether the perceptions and expectations of students reflected the tenets of postmodernism. When the sub-factors of MRM were examined, it was determined that in summarizing the meaning of each factor with reference to the sub-factors the kernel was found to be "respect", "power-sharing" and "helping them see the bigger picture". These sub-factors embody the seven qualities which represent what I have posited as some of the critical requirements of leadership in a postmodern era and which are consistent with the tenets of postmodernism, namely, consultation and shared leadership; inclusion and participation; respect for otherness/diversity; tolerance of, and patience, with ambiguity; shared decision making; and affirmation of diverse giftedness.

Exploring Proposition MRM against the Backdrop of the Basic Philosophies of Selected Caribbean Thinkers

Sir Shridath Ramphal

Sir Shridath Ramphal is former chancellor of the University of the West Indies and the long-serving Commonwealth secretary general from 1975 to 1990.

As I reflected on a slice of the philosophy and leadership ideology of Sir Shridath, I recall his chancellor's address at the 1990 graduation ceremony in which he spoke of the call to West Indian leaders to advance the *integration* project. Sir Shridath was perhaps the epitome of the practice of regional integration. His refrain in that address were the words "Is WI" (meaning the West Indies but a play on the collective pronoun "we"). Pregnant in that call was the assertion that the solution to the problems of the region was to be found in a collective effort and shared leadership.

In seeking to examine the underlying philosophy of Sir Shridath I was able to establish, through the help of the Ramphal Institute, that one of the key elements of his leadership was his adoption of the technique of using expert groups to make recommendations to governments. This approach differed quite remarkably from others which rely on some lone czar to solve particular problems facing governments. Thus, what Sir Shridath sought to emphasize was the importance of engaging a collective consciousness in seeking to find solutions. Thus WI/WE was a statement of the many being a collective one, and thus the need to see the resolution to the problems as being found in the WI and the WE.

The key elements of Sir Shridath's basic philosophy that stand out are the articulation of the view that leadership is a collective endeavour and thus his belief in the collective wisdom, and the trust he has in the capacity of Caribbean leaders to work collaboratively to solve the problems faced by the region.

Professor Rex Nettleford

The late Rex Nettleford served as a vice chancellor of the University of the West Indies from 1996 to 2004, but prior to assuming leadership of the university he had distinguished himself as an outstanding scholar. His most cogent articulation of what I would call his postmodern ideology is his classic *Mirror Mirror*. Nettleford was a bridgehead of a postcolonial intellectual and activist who sought to demonstrate that the narratives of people of the "third world" were not inferior to that of people of the colonial dynasties of Europe. Nettleford contended that rather than being inferior, the philosophical notions of the Third World contrast, but are equal to, the narratives and grand theories of western Europe and its political and economic allies. Nettleford acknowledged that the work of developing a competitive and convincing counternarrative was a work in progress but a task that was vitally necessary as part of the process of preparing the people of the Caribbean for participation in the political, social and economic processes of their generations. Nettleford contended that the people of the Caribbean should be unrelenting in seeking to have a voice in the dialogues about the future of their society and to resist attempts by the powerful to define the destiny of the region.

The Most Honourable Michael Manley

The legacy and contribution of Michael Manley to the development of Jamaica and the Caribbean is a matter of continuous debate. I do not intend to attempt to address the controversies. Rather, I seek to focus on one important element of his contribution that I think the majority of people would agree is without question, namely his contribution to correcting the social imbalances in the Jamaican society in the 1970s and in particular the policies he pursued that created opportunities for members of the lower social classes to have had access to education.

Manley was in many respects a postmodernist who exercised the courage, particularly during his first stint as prime minister (1972–80), to challenge the powers of Europe and North America in seeking to shape a new Caribbean reality built around economic equity, sovereignty, power sharing and sustainable leadership. In his seminal work *A Voice at the Workplace,* Manley articulates a philosophy of worker participation and inclusion in decision making and outlined a formula for workers' share in the ownership of the means of production. At the heart of his philosophy was the view that workers bring to the economic development process not just their labour but their ideas, the engagement of which would in all likelihood serve to advance the profitability of companies and the prosperity of the nation.

In his controversial work *Up the Down Escalator,* Manley (1987) examines the constraints and strictures faced by fragile and emerging Third World economies as a result of the dictates of the international economic arrangements which he argues are largely defined by the International Monetary Fund (IMF) and the World Bank. Manley's basic thesis is that Caribbean, and other developing countries, should not accept the dictates of the IMF and other western financial entities as the only viable approaches to development but that its leaders should be courageous enough to challenge the conventional wisdom of trickle-down economics, dispute the inherited ideology of the inherent purity and objectivity of the market, and question the assumed inerrancy and infallibility of structural adjustment. The underlying themes of *Up the Down Escalator* were a concern for the socio-economic jam and debt-ridden condition in which Third World countries were faced and the urgency with which the Caribbean needed to exercise the courage to articulate an alternative narrative to those that were being advanced by the Western powers with respect to the paths to economic stability and prosperity.

The perspectives of Ramphal, Nettleford and Manley reflect a sharp insight into the characteristics and callings of Proposition MRM. Proposition MRM promotes inclusiveness, power sharing, respect, egalitarianism and an approach to pedagogy which emphasizes constructivism. The embrace of these characteristics is reflected in the views of Ramphal, Nettleford and Manley.

Proposition MRM is based on the principle of leadership by example and accountability; respect for others and the inclusion of others in the decision-making process; and inclusive of empowerment by way of motivation that is informed by insight into, and understanding of, the bigger picture. Thus, the call to Caribbean leaders in a postmodern era is one that stresses that leadership is a collective endeavour. Proposition MRM is predicated on the notion that the leader is not the only wise and capable person in the group; thus, the call is for a collective approach in seeking to find solutions to the problems facing an organization or country. Leadership in a postmodern era requires that Caribbean leaders eschew dependence on theories and solutions developed in other contexts and in other eras, which are informed by others' epistemologies, and instead pursue with confidence a WI epistemology which seeks to address the challenges WE face as a region. This will require that WE in the WI become more audacious in defining our own epistemologies developing our own theories.

Through the education reforms of the seventies Jamaica was able to assert its place in the global dialogue on economic priorities. Participation in a global dialogue meant that Jamaica was shaping a narrative that could potentially compete with other narratives for space and attention. The call to a continuing development and engagement of a narrative that can compete for space and attention remains relevant for today's, and indeed tomorrow's, Caribbean.

5 | Proposition MRM and Educational Leadership in the Caribbean

Proposition MRM as an Ethical Construct

The constructs of modelling, respect and motivation (MRM) are to be viewed as elements of leadership behaviour, leadership duty and leadership responsibility and, as such, become issues of ethics. The leader has a duty to act in the best interest of the organization and model the behaviours that they expect others to display. The expectation that the leader will model the conduct expected of those they lead is a moral duty. A responsible leader will, on most occasions, seek to make decisions that benefit the majority of members of the organizations rather than the minority. These are the claims of Proposition MRM and in that regard, Proposition MRM is informed by two main ethical theories: deontology and utilitarianism.

The word deontology is derived from the Greek words for duty (*deon*) and science (or study) of (*logos*) and refers to the process of determining those choices which are morally required, forbidden or permitted. Deontology, therefore, provides a context for guiding and assessing our choices of what we ought to do or have done.

Utilitarianism is based on the principle of seeking the highest good for the largest number of people. There are two types of utilitarianism: act utilitarianism and rule utilitarianism. These types of utilitarianism are not opposites as they are approaches that may be taken in a given situation. In this regard a leader may, in a given set of circumstances, be governed by act utilitarianism and in a separate set of circumstances approach the issue using rule utilitarianism.

Act utilitarianism is an approach to ethical decision making that emphasizes that the better choice (when faced with a dilemma which involves taking a course of action that benefits the majority versus one that benefits the minority) is to do what benefits the majority. Under this approach, the assumption is that the decision is being taken to help the majority regardless of personal feelings or the societal constraints. Rule utilitarianism, however, takes into account the law and is concerned with fairness. Thus, the added benefits of rule utilitarianism are that it values justice and includes beneficence at the same time.

One of the features of a postmodern era is easy access to information and new and creative ways of verifying the accuracy of information. In an earlier era, when information was not storable for long periods and then easily accessible at the time of need, it was difficult to hold leaders accountable for what they say. This is no longer the case and as such responsible ethical conduct, expressed in behaviour modelling, is not only a duty but also the sensible thing to do if a leader wishes to remain credible. Proposition MRM embraces the fact that stakeholders in an organization can have easier access to information and can shape their advocacy positions more sharply as well as hold leaders accountable more effectively. Proposition MRM is, therefore, to be seen as promoting a culture of ethical awareness that summons leaders to duty and action in the interest of the majority. The latter notion is predicated on the view that the best decisions are more often than not those in which a cross section of stakeholders had an input.

The issue of modelling is also predicated on what Aristotle describes as the maxims. Aristotle suggests that duty ethics represents the imposition of an obligation on people to act in such ways that their actions may form the basis of maxims. In simple terms what this suggests is that one of the bases on which a leader may determine the ethical status of an action is to consider whether or not that action could be defensible or advance the well-being of the community if it were to become the norm. Modelling may be seen simply as the portrayal of behaviours that are the desired norms.

The element of respect is also a distinctively an ethical issue. Leaders have a duty to respect others. This duty is articulated by the eighteenth century philosopher Immanuel Kant, who recommends that at all times we should treat human beings as ends and not as means. The centrepiece of Kant's ethical theory is the claim that all individuals are owed respect just because they are persons – that is, free rational beings. To be a person is to have a status and worth that is unlike that of any other kind of being: it is to be an end in itself with dignity. Thus, the only response that is appropriate to such a being is respect. Respect comes from the Latin word *recipecere,* which means to see the other as the other is and not as one wishes the other to be. Respect, then, is an acknowledgement in attitude and conduct of the dignity of individuals. The obligation to show respect is what Kant calls a categorical imperative and one element of that categorical imperative for educational leaders is inclusion. The act of inclusion is based on the view that success in pursuing the goals of the organization is predicated on the contribution of others who have the will and capacity to contribute meaningfully to the attainment of those goals. In the simple terms, the leader needs others if they are to be successful in leading the organization.

Porath (2015) argues that being respectful benefits everyone. In a study of nearly twenty thousand employees around the world, Porath found that employee commitment and engagement have their greatest chances of success when employees feel respected. Porath contends that no other leadership behaviour had a bigger effect on employees across the outcomes measured and found that being treated with respect was more important to employees than recognition and appreciation, communicating an inspiring vision or providing useful feedback. In this regard then, respect is not only a moral imperative it is the sensible thing to do.

Motivation is a form of energy that is needed for production and productivity. The greatest source of motivational energy is, I suggest, a consciousness about process and expected outcomes and their relationship to be bigger picture or larger purpose. When people can see their place in the total patchwork, they are better able to make decisions on how to relate and find the other resources needed to help them to decide how to engage.

There are two major lessons that may be drawn from the assertion that Proposition MRM is an ethical construct. These may be summarized as follows:

1. Educational systems and policies should be all-inclusive and built on the principle of attaining the best outcomes for the largest number of people.
2. Respect for stakeholders of the organization is fundamental to the success of the organization. This respect manifests itself in engagement in decision making and goal setting.

Proposition MRM as a Pedagogical Construct

A friend of mine once had the following statement on her WhatsApp page: "I facilitate thinking, I engage minds, I listen to questions, I encourage risk I support struggle, I cultivate dreams, I learn every day. I am a teacher."

This is a deeply profound statement which encapsulates in an elegant way the method, modality, meaning, purpose and mission of teaching and learning. In the first instance, the teaching and learning process relies for its effectiveness and sustainability on *critical* thinking or, more pointedly, the capacity to critique. Critiquing means that the critic has not taken what is presented at face value but has gone beyond the surface to probe, to ask questions and to wonder out aloud. I have often shared with students that one of the most exciting expressions to which I look forward to hearing from them contain the words, "I was thinking . . .". Thinking leads to questioning and the asking of some types of questions involve risks. Proposition MRM is predicated on each of these behaviours. I suggest that Proposition MRM is a pedagogical construct on at least four levels.

The first level at which Proposition MRM is a pedagogical construct is that it calls upon, and expects of the teacher the skill of and commitment towards facilitating thinking. This means that the teacher must be a *model* of critiquing. Being a model of critiquing requires the demonstration of at least two dispositions and approaches to pedagogy. In the first place, the teacher should treat the material being presented to students as perspectives, approaches and world views that are subject to question – regardless of the source. One of the pitfalls into which many teachers fall is that of having a default setting of uncritical acceptance of course materials and often ends up transmitting the material to students with the expectation that they will accept the material without exercising the courage to doubt and dispute. Thus, rather than presenting the material in a dogmatic and inflexible manner, an MRM disposition to pedagogy invites teachers to present material with an openness to new and alternative points of view.

The second level at which Proposition MRM invites entry to a new pedagogy is predicated on the expectation that the teacher will not only offer disclaimers about the sources of information and thus leave space for doubt and further reflection but that the teacher will be willing to subject their own strongly held views, convictions and assumptions to dispute and debate by students "to her or his face". This need for teachers to adopt a pedagogical approach which welcomes disputation and debate is informed, among other things, by the reality that fundamentalist thinking as a dominant way of seeing the world has been replaced, to a great extent by more radical, progressive perspectives. The spread and adoption of radical and progressive perspectives are aided by the influence of social media and multiple sources of information. One implication of this new dynamic and its relevance to pedagogy is that students enter a world that is crafted on diversity, characterized by ambiguity, propelled by plurality and steeped in complexity with an orientation to reject prefabricated postulations which are deemed to be out of sync with the realities around them.

The creation of a pedagogical framework of learner disputation, which is one of the premises of Proposition MRM, takes on even greater significance and urgency given the fact that we live in an age in which it is so easy to transmit information to large audiences using multiple media. In the absence of mechanisms for vetting and fact checking before information is placed in the public space, the need for critical thinking takes on enormous significance. If teachers, in their day-to-day engagement with students, behave as though some voices (namely theirs and a few others) are beyond question, then there is the risk that there could be the entrenchment of a disease of uncritical engagement at other levels.

Proposition MRM as a pedagogical construct calls on the teacher to be a model of critical thinking which begins with being self-critical.

Caribbean teachers who share the unfortunate reality of inherited narratives must therefore become more astute, bullish and urgent in seeking to create new knowledge through research and reflection to enable them and their students to acquire perspectives that are more relevant to the contexts within which countries of the Caribbean find themselves. This engagement in research must not be seen, however, as merely designed to make sense of the existing realities but more so to create new realities.

The third level at which Proposition MRM is a pedagogical construct is in relation to the critical element of respect. Respect means to show regard, to listen to, to treat with seriousness, to take account of. Wood (1999) suggests that when one respects another, one is not prone to be oblivious or indifferent to that person, or to ignore or quickly dismiss that person. Respect is then, I submit, a quintessential requirement of the teacher-student relationship. Respect runs along a two-way street, with teacher respecting student and vice versa. Showing respect to students creates the perfect condition for students to learn, as Hughes and Kwok (2007), Eccles, Wigfield and Schiefele (1998), and Ullman (1997) suggest.

The fourth level at which Proposition MRM is a pedagogical construct is based on the direction of its moorings. The modelling of critical thinking and the showing of respect are designed to result in a motivated student ready to explore the complexities of the world. The courage and audacity with which students are willing to take on the issues of their world are dependent on the extent to which they have been enabled to believe in themselves and have grasped an emerging understanding of life beyond school. In the construct of Proposition MRM, motivation is linked to a growing understanding of the larger issues facing an organization and a society.

Proposition MRM, Postmodernism and TVET

Proposition MRM is to be understood as an approach to educational leadership which emphasizes inclusion, power sharing, egalitarianism and respect for diversity. Technical and vocational education and training (TVET) as a mode of educational development is predicated on the belief that all learners can acquire marketable skills and can contribute meaningfully to the development of a society and thus can enjoy the fruits of an inclusive society in which there is equity and equal access to opportunity and the resources required to sustain a healthy life.

The principles of SD are similar in character to those of Proposition MRM and TVET in a number of ways. SD emphasizes inclusion, power sharing, respect for diversity, access to opportunity, sharing of resources and participation in the opportunities for a healthy life. In this regard, then, Proposition MRM, TVET and SD are common principles that inform a particular ideology and approach to leadership.

I suggest that there is a deep relationship between the nature and purpose of TVET and the *spirit* and motif of postmodernism. One important characteristic of TVET is its emphasis on application. TVET is a mode of learning by doing which applies the principles of science, technology, engineering and mathematics. By virtue of its emphasis on applied learning, TVET is naturally a learner-empowerment mode of teaching which requires an inclusive pedagogy while creating the opportunity for acquiring the sensitivities and skills for other-focused problem-solving engagement with one's environment. TVET positions students to become more skilled in finding solutions to the problems in their environment and to be creators of new knowledge.

By virtue of positioning students to be creators and inventors of outputs which reflect application of new knowledge, TVET represents a strong expression of the constructivist element of postmodernism. In this regard, TVET also gives expression to the postmodern assertion that grand narratives are no longer the only source of credible knowledge. The upshot of this is that TVET represents a key pathway for students to be more meaningfully engaged in the enterprise of socio-economic development. In light of this, I suggest that the integration of TVET in the mainstream of the general education system is both inevitable and imperative if the education system is to be more responsive to the demands of a postmodern era.

Innovation is the ultimate measure of applied learning and, as I have indicated earlier, one of the distinguishing features of TVET is its emphasis on learning by doing. This practice-based approach, which admits errors, is an important component of the energy that drives innovation. When learning from error is seen as part of the architecture of innovation, then people experience greater freedom to discover and, in the process, add greater value to the organization (Thompson 2015).

The practice-based TVET curriculum may be viewed as movement from activities in which errors could be tolerated, through to those where mistakes come at a high price, Billett (2013) suggests, and the sequencing of these activities is structured to progressively engage novices in increasingly demanding activities, each requiring incrementally greater levels of skill.

Sweet (2013) posits that China's phenomenal economic success owes much to its use of what Billet describes as the practice-based curriculum. Sweet (2013) traces the evolution of China's education system, noting that it evolved from a relatively underdeveloped apprenticeship system that had existed since the late 1950s, which was abandoned during the Cultural Revolution, to the 1985 decision of the Central Committee of the Communist Party that made the determination that training should precede employment, as Guo and Lamb (2010), cited by Sweet (2013), recall. Since then, Sweet continues, the dominant paradigm in upper-secondary-level vocational education in China has been the "train and place model", in which one to two years of work placement in an enterprise follow two years that are spent in a vocational school (Han 2009; Zhao 2011 as cited by Sweet 2013).

There would, of course, be operational challenges to be overcome such as the limited placement locations in some areas where schools are situated, difficulty in arranging transportation to distant locations, safety issues on some plants, site supervision and just the sheer number of students within a context of a small economy. Ways would need to be found to overcome these and one such would be to redesign schools such that each school has a semi-industrial area and involving parent-teacher associations and the larger community in this endeavour would serve to reduce the stigma attached to TVET. With all students being exposed to TVET, and with improved information dissemination about the scope of TVET and value of the jobs to the economy and with parents on board, the process of integrating TVET into the mainstream of the education system would be well underway.

Morris (2009) asserts that policies to guide the development and implementation of technical and vocational education and training (TVET) are critical if maximum benefits are to be derived from this type of education. Noting that TVET is now widely accepted by developing countries as a critical tool in their efforts to eradicate poverty and enhance human development, Morris (2009) cites Labelle (2005), who advances recommendations for formulating policies for information and communication technologies (ICTs). Among the recommendations advanced by Labelle are the need to promote public-private partnerships, adopt participatory approaches and take account of local market needs.

One of the vestiges of the colonial era, from which the Caribbean is seeking to, and must, emerge, is the seemingly engrained notion of scarcity. This scarcity manifested itself in the early post-independence era of the 1960s when the education system was characterized by limited access for the majority. There were only a few high schools and thus only the very privileged were able to have access. The situation was worse with college and university places. Much of the educational offerings were predicated on white collar professional skills in traditional areas of law, medicine, education and office administration. One of the results of this arrangement was that the thinking was infused in the society that improved life predicated on a traditional high school, college and university education. The socio-economic transformation of the countries of Southeast Asia has proven that a solid education system can be built around TVET. The transformation of Southeast Asian economies through TVET provides a template for development for the Caribbean. One of the lessons that this transformation has taught is that improvement in life chances and the quality of life for the masses of the poor can be attained, and the economies of the Caribbean can, like those in Southeast Asia, become economies with surplus.

Morris (2009) suggests that this problem of scarcity be overcome if countries make TVET a critical component of their proposed socio-economic transformation process. Citing the experience of countries such as Singapore, Malaysia, Japan, of Southeast Asia and Botswana in Africa, Morris asserts that these countries, and in particular Singapore, are examples of how a vision of development that includes TVET, and determination and strong leadership can result in transformation which, I would add, seeks a triumph of abundance of opportunity where scarcity existed.

The importance of vision and determined leadership of which Morris (2009) speaks is supported by Hutton (2009), who laments the weak performance of vocational programmes in schools, which result from, among other things, lack of adequate facilities and quality instructors. It is self-evident that if there were a vision of how the education system and the economy of a country can be transformed through the use of TVET, then greater attention would be paid to fundamentals such as the adequacy of facilities and the quality of facilitators.

Proposition MRM, TVET and SD

UNESCO asserts that the term TVET is used to describe technical and vocational education that is comprehensive in nature and refers to those aspects of the educational process involving, in addition to general education, the study of technologies and related sciences, and the acquisition of practical skills, attitudes, understanding and knowledge relating to occupations in various sectors of economic and social life (UNESCO 2005).

One of the seminal contributions to the discussion on how to achieve the integration of TVET in the mainstream of the education system is a 2013 UNESCO publication entitled *Revisiting Global Trends in TVET: Reflections on Theory and Practice*. In this volume, which boasts a number of compelling papers, Majumdar, head of UNESCO-UNEVOC and editor of the publication, notes that through its TVET Strategy (2010–15), UNESCO explicitly recognizes the value of TVET in addressing a host of issues, such as youth unemployment and socio-economic inequalities. Specifically, he argues, the TVET strategy aims to "strengthen its assistance to Member States to improve their TVET systems and practices . . . by promoting long-term solutions based on an inclusive and rights-based approach"

(UNESCO 2013). Decades before UNESCO's 2013 publication, there were other seminal, visionary and sustained efforts at realizing the integration of TVET in the mainstream of education systems. These include:

1. The 1974 affirmation by the United Nations of the critical importance of TVET to national development and the issuing of the *Revised Recommendation concerning Technical and Vocational Education.*
2. The staging of various TVET congresses globally, the first being held in Germany in 1987; the second in Seoul, South Korea in 1999; and the third in Shanghai in 2012.

The theme for the 2012 congress, "Building Skills for Work and Life", was particularly instructive as it sought to highlight the centrality of TVET to all facets of human comfort and survival. The congress further enhanced the debate on the role of TVET in the twenty-first century, providing a forum for discussion on the challenges faced by the TVET systems and the appropriate responses to them. One of its important outcomes of the congress was the production of a set of key recommendations to governments and other TVET stakeholders in UNESCO member states, presented under seven strands (known as the Shanghai Consensus, UNESCO 2012).

1. Enhancing the relevance of TVET
2. Expanding access and improving quality and equity
3. Adapting qualifications and developing pathways
4. Improving the evidence base
5. Strengthening governance and expanding partnerships
6. Increasing investment in TVET and diversifying financing
7. Advocating for TVET

While the recommendations of the Shanghai Consensus are explicit and compelling and may be deemed to provide a framework for action by governments that are keen on strengthening the role of TVET, a slow pace of action of some governments in the Caribbean requires that an analysis of possible contributory factors to the reticence and seeming equivocation be explored.

An important feature of the way forward, and part of the reason the integration of TVET in the mainstream of the education system is so vital, is that it constitutes an important component of SD. The United Nations has identified seventeen goals of SD which collectively define the concept of SD. The goals of SD include the elimination of poverty and hunger, and the improvement in the conditions of health and well-being, quality education, gender equality, peace and justice for all with efforts directed at alleviating the condition of those who are most adversely affected by the disparities in the distribution of resources. Thus economic, social and environmental health is the ultimate goal of SD.

In its landmark and defining statement on SD, the Organization for Economic Cooperation and Development (OECD) in the publication entitled *Sustainable Development: Critical Issues,* points out that

(a) The global nature of many of the most pressing development challenges makes it imperative that countries build strong coalitions to address issues of common concern. Among the suggestions advanced by the OECD is the need for more inclusive decision making.
(b) The objectives of sustainable development require that countries seek to establish the institutional and technical capacity to interrogate proposed developmental undertakings and therefore critically assessing these proposals with respect to their economic, environmental and social implications and to formulate and implement appropriate policy responses.

The creation of more inclusive systems of decision making and the deployment of critical assessment capabilities require, as the OECD suggests:

(c) An integrated framework of effective institutions is essential for sustainable development with significant participation of civil society in policy making and implementation,

and of vital importance:

(d) The provision of support for, and the facilitation of, technological development which emphasizes innovation-led growth which integrates sustainability into the economic and research systems.

These elements of SD require, for their effectiveness, a culture that is built on the principles of transformational leadership. The single most critical variable required for SD is the collective will of the people of a community to behave in ways that preserve, expand and renew the shared natural and social resources. For this to be achieved, every citizen has to become a believer and actor. A key responsibility of leadership is to provide information in ways that inform, influence and inspire and having done so to facilitate inclusive decision making. The principle of inclusive decision making is a key tenet of SD and a primary requirement of a postmodern era.

SD, therefore, requires the creation of institutional systems to support and maintain the inclusive decision making, ongoing stakeholder consultation, respect for diversity and collective decision making. These *systems* need to be integrated if they are to support each other.

TVET and SD, as well as Proposition MRM and SD, may be said to be the two sides of the same coin. TVET like SD is dependent on innovation-led growth in order to be effective. TVET's purpose is to find solutions that enable us to live comfortably and prosperously. To achieve this, TVET practitioners must be constantly innovating. If the innovations pursued by TVET do not take account of the need for preservation, renewal and expansion, then the resources of the environment from which TVET draws will eventually be depleted and as such would be at odds with the requirements of SD. In this regard, the sustainable pursuit of TVET requires an inclusively developed policy framework that carries a shared political commitment. SD is built on the principles of consultation, shared leadership, inclusive decision making, citizen participation, respect for otherness and embrace of diversity.

Perhaps one of the most important socio-political realities, the reduction of which is shared by TVET, SD and Proposition MRM, is the issue of inequality. Proposition MRM, which posits a new understanding of transformational leadership stresses shared power, egalitarianism and the pursuit of a shared agenda for the benefit of the majority. In this regard, Proposition MRM as an ethical construct embraces the principle of utilitarianism. SD asserts that one of the major contributors to the economic impoverishment of large numbers of people across the globe is inequality. SD further contends that the improvement in the living conditions, and prospects for prosperity, for marginalized groups require a rebalancing of the modes and system of access to, and distribution of, resources required for health and wealth. Thus, SD and Proposition MRM go hand in hand.

TVET represents an approach to education and development which promulgates an educational ideology and methodology that increases the probability for more people, particularly the marginalized, to participate in economic development, thereby reducing poverty and inequality. TVET can serve as a strategy to reduce poverty and inequality by providing unemployed youth with the skills, knowledge and perspectives needed for developing self and society. The place/status of many of our young people is still determined by their position in a postcolonial society still structured around race, colour and class. The resulting low self-confidence, self-esteem issues can be addressed by TVET providing them with the technological skills for "decent work". TVET can thus lead in addressing the inequities/social justice issues that limit development in a sustainable way.

TVET's potential to contribute to the reduction in poverty and inequality is found in the fact that it can lead in promoting the research to support more sustainable solutions that lead to SD challenges. One critical component of the agenda for SD that runs alongside issues such as consultative policymaking and which holds an important key for ending poverty and hunger is alternative energy resources. It is instructive in this regard that chapter 36 of Agenda 21 speaks to vocational training as one of the key components of the strategy to end poverty and hunger.

A radical programme of integration of TVET and the matching of skills to the needs of the market place must be led by the universities. This strategy is an absolute necessity for achieving economic development and growth, as the experience of China, Germany, France, Indonesia, India and Pakistan, among others, have shown.

The integration TVET in the mainstream of the education system has been assessed by UNESCO as being a vital step to improving students' chances of success in the world of work as well as strengthening the economic performance of countries. Countries such as China, Denmark, Finland, Germany, Indonesia, Singapore, Sweden and the United Kingdom that have taken steps to integrate TVET in the mainstream of their education systems have seen significantly greater performance in their students and in their economies than have countries that are yet to achieve integration. Most Caribbean countries have not been successful in integrating TVET in the mainstream of the education system.

If countries, particularly in the Caribbean, are to be successful in integrating TVET in the mainstream of the education system, a number of fundamental requirements must be satisfied. These requirements, broadly speaking, involve consensus among the various stakeholders (inclusive of policymakers, parents, teachers, students and donor agencies), as well as collaborative engagements between and among various sets of stakeholders at different stages of the integration (and consolidation of the integration) process.

Caribbean countries depend heavily on foreign direct investment for their growth and development of their economies, whether for the building of resorts or mining bauxite and other minerals. In a number of instances, the proposed investments are in conflict with the research findings and recommendations of environmentalists based on the analyses of these environmentalists that some proposed developments are in keeping with SD. While investment decisions are sometimes stayed, there is often an ongoing worry that a particular government will give in the demands of foreign investors to the detriment of their people and the environment.

A number of recent cases in Jamaica illustrate this dilemma. For clarity, it is to be recalled that a dilemma is a situation in which two legitimate (lawful and ethical options) present themselves but a choice must be made in favour of one and thus at the expense of the other.

The dilemmas of which I speak were the (then) proposed construction of a hotel in the vicinity of river on the north coast. Despite opposition from the environmental lobby groups that development was given environmental permits to proceed. More recently, in 2016, there was the controversy on the removal of sand from one parish to another as part of the construction of a hotel. A stop order was placed on the sand removal by the agency with the authority to do so but later rescinded by the minister with responsibility for the environment, who cited economic considerations for the rescinding of the stop order.

Although no development permits have yet been issued for Jamaica's Cockpit Country, environmentalists remain suspicious that this may occur and that bauxite mining may soon take place there. Thus, the clash of economic developmental imperatives with environmental needs considerations remain a present and potent dilemma for many Caribbean countries.

The challenge that faces Caribbean countries in respect to environmental SD is that of crafting viable economic alternatives to the proposed development proposals of foreign investors in order to take account of SD imperatives. Having devised those alternatives, Caribbean countries will then need to negotiate with prospective investors to ensure that development approaches are consistent with their philosophies of SD. It is that determination to negotiate that will, among other things, be a mark of maturity and a level of self-confidence that arises from a capacity to articulate a defined ideology that takes account of one's history and current reality.

It is my further suggestion that Caribbean universities have a key role to play in crafting SD ideas and solutions that draw on insights from TVET. Unless Caribbean universities are able to use the principles of TVET (which as a practice uses the principles of science, technology, engineering and mathematics) to inform development alternatives that take account of the peculiarities, needs and history of the Caribbean, our universities will be failing in their duty to ensure that research outputs support the creation of solutions that drive socio-economic development.

Proposition MRM as a Framework for Long-Term Thinking

Leaders must possess a vision of where they wish to take their organization and use that vision to inspire others. Inspiration is the state of having been sold on a brilliant idea that leads to passion and commitment to a large cause that is life changing. Commitment to a large life-changing cause is what is meant by motivation and one is motivated when one is able to hold in view that bigger picture.

Motivational or inspirational leadership, therefore, is about helping others see the bigger picture. This is the responsibility of every leader. One of the means by which this is achieved is by bringing followers into the mainstream and sharing with them pertinent information that would enable them to engage their personal energies and interests in a manner that will advance the goals of the self, others and the organization.

It has long been recognized and argued in several works, including that of Mayo (1933), that the capacity to motivate others is an important and indispensable quality in leadership and, as has been shown in the foregoing discussion, in the process of defining leadership (in the context of schools), insufficient emphasis has been placed on the fact that students *expect* their leaders (principals and teachers) to motivate them. It is not surprising, therefore, that the quality of the leadership offered by teachers and principals is measured to a considerable degree by the extent to which they provide motivation.

Schooling is not an end in itself. It is the means to many ends. Ultimately, therefore, the true measure of how well the energies and interests of students have been engaged (that is, how well motivated they are) is to be found in the extent to which the experience of schooling is deemed by them to be preparing them for life after school. One of the ways in which school is expected to prepare students for life after school is through enabling them to develop the capacity to find answers to the realities and peculiarities of their own world. Finding answers to the peculiarities of one's world requires the development of one's own "epistemology". Keunzli-Monard and Keunzli (2004) emphasize that in a postmodern world, reality is constructed. They contend that the notion of finding pre-existing truths is a premodern idea whose unsoundness has been exposed by the rapid pace of technological innovation, the expansion and commoditization of knowledge and other developments that impact on open systems. Lyotard, whose ideas are supported by Keunzli-Monard and Keunzli, argues that the various "master-narratives" of progress such as positivist science, Marxism and structuralism had failed and were defunct as methods of achieving progress. Lyotard, therefore, saw the need to develop a new approach to the search for knowledge.

Proposition MRM as a Justification for Students' Voices in the Development of Educational Policy

One of the key contentions of Proposition MRM is the claim that SD is linked to a policy and strategy of inclusiveness. This concept is articulated in Agenda 21 and the United Nations Sustainable Development Goals, among other authorities. One dimension of this notion of inclusiveness which is not sufficiently emphasized is the inclusion of the voices of students.

Allport (1937) may be credited as one of the first thinkers to have advanced the view that human beings by nature desire to be involved in decisions that affect their well-being. There is no evidence that Allport had students or juveniles in mind when he made this assertion, but when examined in the context of Proposition MRM it may be declaratively stated that students too desire to be consulted on issues that affect them. This need for broad-based consultation as a function of SD has been accepted as a non-negotiable element of credible leadership and ideal practice in policymaking. One of the questions invited by this assertion is whether, and to what extent, policymakers, whether in the Caribbean or elsewhere, undertake the kind of inclusive policy decision-making approach that welcomes students.

Freire (1970), in his seminal work *Pedagogy of the Oppressed,* articulated the need for an approach to schooling which was based on a pedagogy of inclusion. An important interpretation of Freire's thinking is that a non-inclusive pedagogy (that is, one which gives space the voice of the teacher) is inherently an oppressive pedagogy. This pedagogy is oppressive for, among other things, the fact that it inhibits expression and the sharing of ideas and thus runs counter to the purpose of learning, which is to liberate. Freire's assessment of the relationship between teacher and student is that it presumes the superiority of the teacher, who possesses a bank of information, pouring knowledge into the mind of the empty and ignorant student. The commoditization of knowledge, which was not as widespread as in Freire's time, demonstrably rubbishes the notion that the teacher possesses knowledge that the student does not possess. Given the access that students, of all ages now have to knowledge, the role of teacher has morphed extensively into being that of a co-interpreter, who is on journey of discovery like their students. The need to give space to students to share the pieces of knowledge they possess as well as to offer their own interpretation of the knowledge shared in the learning space is the new frontier of knowledge which Vygotsky (1978) compellingly articulated even before the notion of knowledge superhighways were conceptualized.

Freire's theory of pedagogy may be further interpreted to be posing the question of the value proposition of school and schooling and this value proposition may be read into Illich's (1970) notion of deschooling society. Illich suggests that schooling misleads the poor by confusing process with substance, grade advancement with education, certificate with competence and service in the place of value. The upshot of this, according to both Illich and Freire, is that the interests of the poor are subjugated to the interests of the oppressive economically powerful. The pervasiveness and dominance of the interests of the economically powerful is what has led in part to global initiatives such as Agenda 21, various development goals and the mainstreaming of TVET as part of the general education system. One of the core elements that these initiatives have in common is their objective of giving voice to the marginalized.

Beckett, Glass and Moreno (2013), speaking in the mode of Freire, and exposing some of the inequities that are characteristic of many societies, advance a pedagogy of community building. Community and community building are predicated on the philosophy of creating space for all. The critique being offered here, as articulated in Proposition MRM, is that the all has often not included students.

This pedagogy of community building, which is predicated on inclusiveness, has not been a successful global project as students in many parts of the world continue to protest exclusion and, given racial and economic disparities, the exclusionary features of education systems and educational policymaking has affected some students more than others. This is evidenced, for example, in the work of Bozelek and Zembylas (2017), who lament the continued inequities in higher education in post-apartheid South Africa which has led to movements such as #FeesMustFall. These inequities are evident in other places such as the United States and the United Kingdom with protests such as #StudentBlackOut. The 2018 students' protests in the United States, which were triggered by the school shootings in Parkland, Florida, and the teachers' of Kentucky, demanding reversals of policies that are deemed unfavourable to students, not only highlighted the problem of exclusionary practices in policymaking, but more so illustrate the critical importance of inclusion.

The student-led protests across the United States following the Parkland shootings were assessed by many in the media to have been one of the most, if not the most-successfully mobilized protests by children. A large part of the explanation for the success of the protests was the skilful use of social media. The central claim of this protest was a demand for students' fears and safety to be taken into account in making changes to gun-control laws. Underlying this claim was the fundamental principle of the right to be heard and taken into account, as Allport (1937) contends. The ingredients of Proposition MRM, understood in its call for inclusivity, diversity, community and MRM's relationship to empowerment and SD, are the overarching themes of movements such as #FeesMustFall and #StudentBlackOut and, latterly, the Parkland-inspired protests and teachers' protests.

Some lessons to be drawn from the complex of ideas from Allport, Illich and Freire or two to three generations ago, and the protest movements of 2015 and onwards, are inclusiveness as a strategy of SD, community building and policymaking needs to be defined and consciously presented as referring to all classes and ages of people, and with reference to educational leadership and educational policymaking must include students.

At their thirteenth biennial conference in 2017 in Jamaica, under the theme "Envisioning Future Education: Cross-Disciplinary Synergy, Imperatives and Perspective", the Schools of Education of the University of the West Indies dedicated half a day for conversations with high-school students. This decision was driven by the determination that a credible plan for the future of education could not be crafted without the involvement of students, given that they know the needs and aspirations of their peers better than any adult expert. The credibility of the Schools and the University of the West Indies itself will depend in part on the degree to which its policies and programmes have taken account of the volume of insights and ideas that were generated by students.

Excursus: Overcoming TVET's Misconceptions about TVET and Its Presumed Unattractiveness

Winch (2013) has taken on the issue of the relative attractiveness of TVET. In exploring this, he clarifies that when he speaks of "attractiveness" he is addressing the preferability of TVET compared with alternatives. He explains that the notion of preferability means different things to different stakeholders. At the individual level (whether student or parent), it is the preferability of TVET as opposed to, for example, direct engagement in the labour market or the pursuit of higher education. For employers and trade unions, it is a question of who gets employed and in relation to what skills, while at the level of government policy, it is a question of which alternative will likely receive government spending support – TVET or higher education.

The roots of the perceived unattractiveness of TVET go back over several centuries as Winch (2013) notes, arguing that historically, education was about exposure to the humanities and training targeted those who were required to provide services to the ruling class. TVET, which focuses on training, was therefore classified as being for those who were to perform menial tasks. Winch notes that sometimes, for a relatively favoured few, TVET was in the form of a formal apprenticeship with a contractual agreement, but for the vast majority of the world's population, informal workplace learning, or an extended informal apprenticeship was the most that they could expect.

Even in countries that have made significant economic progress through an advanced TVET programme, there are still perceptions of the unattractiveness of TVET. Ratnata (2013) notes that various efforts have been made by a number of Southeast Asian countries, including his home country Indonesia, to improve the image and attractiveness of TVET. In lamenting the fact that TVET is still not perceived to be as valuable as general education, he notes that in China, Indonesia and South Korea upper-middle-class children are almost certainly to be advised to choose general education in order to pursue their goals in higher education. He observes that a similar situation exists in most of the member countries of the European Union, where parents prefer to send their sons and daughters to general education or university rather than to TVET. As a result of this, vocational schools are still considered second-class and not as attractive as general schools.

Jules (2012), in a paper entitled "Promoting the Attractiveness of TVET in the Context of Secondary Education Reform", which he presented at the 2012 Shanghai Congress, speaking from the context of the Caribbean reality, also laments the perceptions that exist towards TVET, noting that TVET has historically been positioned as a "second chance" wherein students who have not done well academically are shoved into TVET, and are thus seen as academic underachievers. This practice he contends serves to reinforce negative notions of TVET. The associated negative notions, therefore, lead many employers and parents to see TVET careers as low wage and low skilled. These notions are at odds with the real nature of TVET, which has been further transformed by digital technologies. Jules suggests that the solution to this negative perception of TVET lies in the establishment of a TVET Policy Framework.

Simiyu (2009), in a case study of a technical institute in Kenya designed to investigate the factors that influence the attractiveness, found that teamwork among all stakeholders (teachers, parents, students and the community) was a necessary ingredient for successful institutional performance and the ultimate attractiveness of its programmes. He found further that the quality of leadership offered by the principal and the marketing of the effectiveness of the marketing of the programme were vital to the success of the programme.

Various perspectives are implied, and others explicit, that indirectly or directly address the issue of the unattractiveness of TVET. Implicitly the argument is simple: find ways to make TVET more attractive.

One of the explicit strategies that was identified as a tool for overcoming the unattractiveness of TVET is policy. Tikly (2013), in seeking to examine the relevance of a human capability and social-justice approach for understanding the role of TVET in relation to development, notes that there are somewhat contrasting emphases between financial institutions such as the World Bank in relation to policies to promote TVET and that of entities such as UNESCO. He posits that financial institutions principally see TVET as an investment in human capital and as a means for supporting economic growth while UNESCO has been linked to a more human-centred view of TVET as a means for supporting SD. He contends that an appreciation of these contrasting perspectives is critical to how countries seek to engage either entity when seeking support for efforts designed to integrate TVET in the mainstream education system. Implicit in Tikly's argument is the view that the policy lever, as an instrument of strengthening the role of TVET, particularly for developing countries, requires sensitivity to the funding and programme priorities of donor and lending agencies.

Tikly notes that the African Union's Plan of Action for the Second Decade of Education (2006–15) recognizes the importance of TVET as a means of empowering individuals to take control of their lives and the defined strategy is the integration of vocational training into the general education system. This is a clear example of leadership by way of policy support.

Papua New Guinea which launched its TVET Policy in 2005 pointed to the importance of policy if a country is to realize the benefits of TVET. Noting that a vibrant, responsive, effective and efficient TVET system is an integral part of the country's development strategy, the policy seeks to ensure the alignment of efforts towards Papua New Guinea's economic directions and national training priorities. The ownership of curriculum content, the policy notes resulted from participation by stakeholders in its framing.

The ministers of education of the African Union, in their 2007 policy framework document "Strategy to Revitalize TVET in Africa", identify a number of priority areas among the economies of the participating nations to which TVET needed to be linked in terms of the relationship between TVET and general education as well as TVET and the needs of the labour market, thus emphasizing that a key pillar of TVET's mainstreaming lies in the extent to which it is linked at the policy level to priorities of the government. The need for these linkages is reinforced in the work of Navneet Boodhai (n.d.), who, in her concept paper on the development of a strategic plan for vocational education services in the Caribbean Community, found that a major problem facing the development of a strong vocational sector was fragmentation, which is the result of the absence of policy. This problem, she contends, emanates in part from weak or inappropriate institutional arrangements such as the absence of a TVET council, a matter some countries, such as Barbados, have begun to address with the setting up of a TVET council.

The use of policy to drive governmental action has two main purposes – alignment of a proposed set of actions to government's priorities and commitment to those courses of action through budgetary support. Such alignment is achieved through strategies such as those used in Korea, where the ministries dealing with TVET are the Ministry of Employment and Labour, the Ministry of Education and the Ministry of Trade, Industry and Energy. The policy underpinning for these alignments is found in the Workers Vocational Skills Development Act, the Act on the Promotion of Industrial Education and Industry-Academy-Research Institute Cooperation, the Act on the Promotion of Vocational Education and Training, and the National Technical Qualifications Act.

6 | Educational Leadership and the Future of the Caribbean

Usher, Bryant and Johnston (1997) identify characteristics of modern and postmodern education and suggest that among the features of modernist education systems are controls imposed by the central government, resulting in a one-size-fits-all approach in a teacher-dominated and student-passive environment. A postmodern educational environment, on the other hand, is controlled by communities, as well as diverse and customized, flexible, lifelong learning in focus and student-centred with emphasis placed on students' experience.

McCullum (n.d.) provides an even more intriguing comparison between modern and postmodern education, noting that in the area of knowledge, modernist approaches to education position the teacher as an unbiased and authoritative transmitter of knowledge, as compared to a postmodern view, which conceives of the teacher as a biased facilitator who is a co-creator of knowledge.

In the area of culture, McCullum assesses that modernist educational approaches view culture as something about which students should learn as the school seeks to create or reinforce a common language and culture to facilitate the smoothness of instruction. A postmodern approach to education, on the other hand, speaks about cultures rather than culture and resists attempts are unification and singleness as successful attempts at these result in domination and exploitation.

Briton (1996) offers what he calls a postmodern critique of adult education. He laments what he sees as a "technicist" trend in adult education and calls for an approach of engagement. Briton's critique is similar to that of Edwards and

Usher (1995) who argues that in modernism "useful" knowledge is emancipatory while in postmodernism, knowledge is exchanged on the basis of its value to the consumer. Edwards and Usher (1995) argue that a postmodern sensitivity to the nature of adult education calls for discourse, representation and difference. They assert that adult educators need to recognize the significance of partial perspectives rather than embracing all-encompassing, universal narratives.

Educational Policymaking and the Caribbean Practitioner

Coopey (1995), summarizing the literature on *organizational learning,* cites the works of Garratt (1987), Pedler, Boydell and Burgoyne (1988) and Senge (1990) and concludes that a "learning culture" encourages the development of individuals and the transformation of the organization by nurturing a questioning spirit, experimentation, differences, openness and tolerance of *disequilibrium* (emphasis not in the original). Coopey (1995) notes that unlike the "hero" as leader in traditional, bureaucratic organizations giving directions, the leaders of learning organizations are designers of the learning process, stewards of the vision and managers of the creative tension between what is and what might be. He further argues that learning organizations give more opportunities for employee self-development and self-management within minimum, flexible structures and organic processes which operate spontaneously, guided by a common purpose and shared vision.

Schein (1993) goes even further than the previously mentioned thinkers. He suggests that today's organizations are no longer faced with the issue of management of change, but management of *surprises*. He calls this the challenge of the *greenroom,* which is a situation of existence in which people are forced to disconfirm the notions and assumptions held dearly, thus requiring that new methods of learning be adopted.

Organizational learning, then, is consistent with the principles and conventions of a postmodern era. Implicit in the arguments advanced is the view that the survival and success of organizations in the current era depends on the extent to which organizations can adopt flexible approaches, thrive on chaos, according to Peters (2010), and benefit from the various technologies of thought and information systems which allow all employees to participate in the development of strategy and policy, adding their own data gleaned through their role as environmental scanners. These sources of data, matched by the discursive capacities of employees, build up agency and thus a reputation for persuasiveness. The consequence of this development of agency is that employees (read: students and teachers) become sources of valuable information and insight to the organization.

Leadership in postmodern times is characterized by an openness and responsiveness to diversity of membership needs and expectations; thus, the organization becomes more effective in meeting the needs of its members, or as Sergiovanni (1991) argues; it is leadership that is essentially participatory. Thus, there is a collective ownership of the "means of need-satisfaction". Collective ownership of anything means that community exists.

Adopting the metaphor of community to describe the process of policymaking has enormous implications and locates the chief policymaker as a partner with the other stakeholder, not a superior. This metaphor has implications for the restructuring of the processes by which educational policy is crafted and implemented. The process must be one that is constructed on the basis of a relationship between and among stakeholders within the context of community and shared ownership. Adopting the community metaphor is in itself a political issue and redefines the interpretation of power and authority.

The plural nature of postmodern society means that there are diverse communities existing side by side that share differing values, hopes and interests. There is no way to adjudicate truth claims between communities; all voices have equal right to be heard. Each community is formed by its own common vision, commitment and values. This growing plurality of communities has implications for leadership. Leaders within these communities cannot be those who force a vision from the top down; postmodern people are suspicious of all truth claims. This is true not only in religious and political contexts in which there has historically been a suspicion of absolute claims to truth and knowledge but also in learning communities.

In postmodern sensibility, truth is considered to be a social construction for the sake of maintaining power. Claims for truth must be deconstructed to expose underlying agendas and grabs for power. Therefore, leaders must find *a modus operandi* that is sensitive to this situation. Leaders can no longer be hierarchical and autocratic but rather participatory and dialogic. The task of the leaders is, as the title indicates, building communities with a common centre. Educational leaders must nurture a community that shares a common vision and understanding of the task of education. The leader is no longer the expert but the facilitator. They encourage and facilitate a dialogue in which a common vision will emerge, forming an educational community.

Schools exist to prepare students for the world in which they will be expected to function. Thus, in a world of diversity, the provision of a diverse program is fundamental, but if the school is being shaped and influenced by its environment, then its programmes must reflect the realities of the era in which it exists whether a Victorian, industrial or postmodern era. Noting that the postmodern mind is hostile to predefined approaches, Coopey (1995) argues that the typical teacher (like most other professionals) of the twenty-first century wants to do their own thing. While no organization can function effectively if everyone is doing "his or her thing", the argument being advanced here is that if schools are to win the respect of their followers, they will have to learn new rules about allowing practitioners more freedom to innovate, set their own agendas as interpreted by their varying situations and exercise the judgement they determine is warranted based on their training and experience within broadly defined parameters. Thus, educational policymaking in a postmodern era must be indexed to the principles of organizational learning, openness to surprises, inclusivity, collective ownership, diversity and contextualization.

The School Principal in the Modern Caribbean

The characteristics of educational leadership and the expectations of leaders in a postmodern era contrast those of premodern and modernist times. In the premodern and modernist eras, the principal or "head teacher" managed the school in the way he (very rarely was it a she) saw fit and notions of consultation, engagement, team approach and power sharing were strange, if not altogether anathema. This approach to leadership was accepted as right and proper and any deviation would be regarded as signs of weakness. It would appear that there are a good many such principals in these postmodern times.

Reflecting both a post-behavioural and postmodern ethic, Hallinger (1992) also argues that teachers possess critical information about their students and how they learn (agency). By virtue of possessing this critical information, teachers need discretionary authority to make their own curricular and instructional decisions. Hallinger's views are presented in the context of the role of transformational leadership, which, he notes, focuses on problem finding, problem solving and collaboration with stakeholders with the goal of improving organizational performance. Conley and Goldman (1994), in supporting this position, note that when teachers function in leadership capacities, they shape the goals and cultures of their school. The exclusion of students and student expertise from the discussion on the design and delivery of the learning and leadership enterprise is a consistent limitation in the scientific literature. This book is an attempt to address that deficit.

Heck, Marcoulides and Lang (1991) constructed an instrument to measure the impact of the principal's instructional leadership. Among the dimensions included in this instrument was "defining the school's mission". By focusing on the principal's design of the school's mission, they were giving a place of pre-eminence to the principal that is again reflecting the modernist point of the view of principal as "lord". In this thinking, the principal is set apart in an almost messianic role, a role which is increasingly being denied leaders in a postmodern society. Even the physical position that the principal occupied in the large, open school provided a separation between principals on the one hand and staff and students on the other.

While there has been a tendency to make a distinction between principals' role as that of *administrative* leadership and that of teachers' as being *pedagogical* leadership, there is an emerging vocal voice calling for a return to the days when principals were activity engaged in pedagogical activity and more intimate with the everyday bounces and scrapes of the classroom. Among those who have been making this case are Wanzare and Da Costa (2001), who in their work "Rethinking Instructional Leadership Roles of the School Principal: Challenges and Prospects" argue that the school principal's tasks in meeting the needs and concerns of ever-changing schools are numerous, complex and challenging. They identify thirty-eight major roles of the principal, including creating a visible presence in the school and supervising instructional activities of teachers. They also examine the principal's instructional leadership roles, the major constraints inherent in this role, and strategies for alleviating problems.

Murphy (1990), in a review of the literature on instructional leadership notes that principals in productive schools – that is, schools where the quality of teaching and learning are strong – demonstrate instructional leadership both directly and indirectly. Like other research that gives the principal a place of prominence, Murphy sees the role of the principal as developing the school's mission and goals; coordinating, monitoring and evaluating curriculum; and promoting a climate conducive to learning, among other *centralistic* functions.

Postmodern thinking on leadership is heavily predicated on notions of self-management, participation, flexibility, heterogeneity and cooperation, thus the inappropriateness of the "lone-leader" leadership style in the management of schools in a postmodern era. There has been, however, a "ground-swell" of opposition to the notion of the principal as sole leader. These include Pescuric and Byham (1996), who see leadership in terms of *modelling* appropriate behaviours for others to emulate; Kaye and Jacobson (1996), who stress the issue of *mentoring*; Cusimano (1996), who talks about managers as *facilitators*; and Campion, Papper and Medsker (1996), who found that *team* characteristics were important elements in the leadership styles of successful organizations. Team approaches to leadership are based on notions of self-management, participation, flexibility, heterogeneity and cooperation, they contend.

One of the key considerations that make Proposition MRM relevant to today's schools the fact that all behaviour is learned. If principals, as a normal part of their execution of their roles, practise shared decision making, accountability as a mode of relating, openness to new ideas and enthusiasm for alternative opinions then, sooner rather than later, that way of leading becomes part of the culture of the school. If teachers in turn relate to students in the same ways, then eventually that way of behaving and being becomes entrenched in the psyche of society.

In a similar way, CEOs who avoid top-down leadership go after suggestions from "below", reward those who innovate, refuse to criminalize those who make mistakes, and are patient with the process of shared decision making. In doing so, a leader will be sending a message about how they desire the organization to be. This message will help to define how an organization learns and grows. In time, heads of departments, managers and supervisors will be infused with a certain mindset about the value of consultative leadership, shared power and respect for the perspectives of others within a culture of shared accountability. In other words, a new culture will emerge, and transformational leadership will become a norm.

The role of principals in a postmodern era should be concerned with facilitating teachers' exercise of initiative and responsibility in instructional matters. Rather than the centralistic role ascribed to the principal under conventional notions of instructional leadership, postmodern notions of leadership conceive of an inclusive, participatory approach compatible with competent and empowered teachers. Principals and teachers play a part in forging an effective leadership relationship. Principals must provide opportunities for teacher growth, but teachers are also responsible for seizing those opportunities. The relationship is a reciprocal one. This reciprocity is based on the willingness of those in formal roles to step aside and allow others into leadership roles.

This phenomenon is, by nature, subtle, sometimes almost imperceptible, and is often not apparent except in certain critical incidents that threaten change efforts. In a postmodern era, therefore, the principal holds a position of shared leadership. The success of the school derives its currency from the collective resources of participants. According to Glanz and Neville (1997), principals and teachers discuss alternatives, rather than having the principal issuing directives, and they work together as a community of learners in their service to students. Perhaps the most critical role of the principal in a postmodern era is that of promoting teacher reflection and contribution and facilitating teacher growth. By seeking to foster collaboration and activate a process of continuous inquiry into teaching and learning, the principal attempts to shape a positive organizational culture and contribute to organizational success.

One of the critical skills required of principals is EQ. Goleman (1998) asserts that the rules for work have changed. People are no longer judged merely on the basis of how smart they are or even by their training and expertise, but increasingly by how strong their people skills are – how they handle themselves and others. He contends that this new paradigm of assessing performance and competence has shifted completely from what schools teach children, as academic abilities are no longer emphasized as the sole basis for measuring workplace competence. These new standards take for granted academic abilities and technical know-how, and focus attention on personal qualities such as initiative, empathy, adaptability and persuasiveness.

The implications of the foregoing description of the role of the principal include the following:

1. A principal who is unwilling to share power with teachers will likely be unwilling to share power with students.
2. A principal who practises power sharing with teachers will be in a better position to influence teachers to practise power sharing with students.
3. The position of principals allows them to influence the power-sharing culture of their schools and send signals as to whether the school embraces or rejects notions of inclusiveness, shared responsibility and democracy.

Ultimately, therefore, the attitude of power sharing demonstrated by principals could be a critical ingredient in determining the attitudes that students develop towards power sharing, which is a skill increasingly demanded in a knowledge-based postmodern world. It is against this background that one of the interests of this book is that of determining the perceptions of students in relation to how their teachers and principals use power.

Farkas and Wetlaufer (1996) have argued that different types of leadership styles may be adopted by a CEO and while not addressing the CEO in a school, their insights are helpful and relevant. They identified different types of leadership styles that were typical of past eras. The periods during which these styles were dominant are roughly consistent with the types of leadership approaches that were practised in the age of scientific management through to the postmodern era. These approaches are the box approach, the human-assets approach, the strategy approach, the expertise approach and the change approach.

The box approach is taken by a CEO who believes in tight controls and thus spends most of their time developing policies and procedures that create controls and limit initiative and creativity. This CEO is consumed with understanding variances and deviations from set policies and targets. This approach describes the typical bureaucracy. The human-assets approach, they argue, is based on a belief that the job of the CEO is primarily to impart certain values, attitudes and behaviours to the organization by closely managing the *development* of individuals. A considerable amount of time is, therefore, spent in issues related to human relations. These qualities are similar to those propounded by the human relations theorists.

The strategy approach focuses on creating, testing, designing and implementing strategy. CEOs who use this approach spend a much of their time understanding the external realities of the organization, and thus delegate the day-to-day business of the organization to *trusted* junior officers who possess finely tuned analytical and planning skills. This approach is roughly similar to the behavioural science era with its focus on the impact of variables.

The expertise approach is used by CEOs who believe that their most important responsibility is selecting and *disseminating* within the organization expertise that will give the organization a competitive advantage. These CEOs spend time in activities related to improving expertise and technology while analysing competitors' products and benchmarking. The preferred recruits, in the thinking of these CEOs, are those who possess flexible minds and lack biases. These characteristics share common nuances with the post-behavioural science era, with its emphasis on emergent and non-traditional perspectives.

The change approach is guided by a belief that a CEO's most critical role is to create an environment of continual reinvention, even if such an environment produces confusion and anxiety and incurs some errors. This CEO is not as consumed with products as they are with *process*. Tight controls, strict policy guidelines and a plethora of rules and regulations do not interest this CEO. The thinking of this kind of CEO reflects the features of postmodernism.

I am advancing the proposition that a theory of educational leadership that is sensitive to the expectations of students, is akin to the paradigms of the expertise and change approaches. A "change approach" may be likened to what other scholars have called a "learning culture".

The Teaching and Learning Process: Proposition MRM and the Caribbean Tomorrow

The teaching and learning process in the Caribbean in a postmodern era will be one ideally characterized by collaboration and shared power. Premodern teacher–student engagement is one-way and directional. Postmodern teacher–student engagements are two-way, mutually engaging, mutually informative and collaborative. In premodern teacher-student relationships the teacher dispenses knowledge and the students absorb and later regurgitate and reproduce for the teacher's assessment what was transmitted. Teacher-student engagements which are informed by Proposition MRM embrace controversy and are respectfully combative.

A postmodern approach to teaching and learning is also concerned with how decisions are taken and who takes those decisions. In the art of teaching, teachers can begin to involve students in decision making in ways as basic as how much energy they have to devote to a particular activity or task. Some practitioners may immediately think that such an approach would be open for abuse, as students are likely to look for opportunities to cop out. This default thinking is based on the mistaken view that students are inherently lazy and will welcome any opportunity to shirk work. This is exactly what McGregor (1960) called Theory X in describing how some managers and supervisors see workers.

Postmodern pedagogies differ from others by virtue of emphasizing the importance of the involvement of the learner in the decision-making process as well as challenging the learner to bring their knowledge (however limited in specific ways) to the process of finding new knowledge and gaining insight. Premodern pedagogies emphasize hierarchy and a top-down approach to leadership. In this setting, the leader is all-knowing and is the premier expert at assessing and monitoring teachers' and students' work.

The willingness of people to show respect to others is related to the degree of concern for each other's needs. This is particularly true for the "underdogs" (individuals with less power) in relationships. Thompson (2009) found that the respect that students perceived they had for their principals, was strongly correlated with the level of concern that principals were perceived to show for the concerns of students. This finding suggests that another expectation that students have of their principals is that they should show interest in their concerns. This influenced students' perceptions of whether the principal was a "good" leader.

One of the gender issues facing society today, and markedly so in the Caribbean and North America, is the seeming lack of attention given to the needs and concerns of boys versus girls. My findings in relation to this matter gave cause for reflection. Boys were found to be generally less of the view that their leaders showed interest in their concern than were girls. Approximately 50 per cent of boys were either unsure about or disagreed with the statement that their principal showed concern. The percentage of males who disagreed or strongly disagreed was 39 per cent (26 of 67). This 39 per cent among males is in contrast to 9 per cent of females who disagreed. There were no *strong* disagreements among females compared with 16 per cent of males who strongly disagreed. This finding may be suggesting that girls are being treated with greater care than boys are and opens the discussion on the currently weighty issue of male marginalization.

The contrasts between the expectations and perceptions of boys versus girls is somewhat addressed by Miller's *theory of place*. Miller (1989) suggested that the ratio of males to females in the teaching force may be a contributing factor to how boys see themselves. The disparity, Miller implies, results in a higher incidence of negative self-concept among boys and contributes to a lack of focus, thereby laying the seeds for under-performance and ultimately their marginalization. The situation facing boys may be characterized as one in which their needs for things of value are not being satisfied, resulting in their having greater levels of discontent. One of the needs that all children have is for positive images of their possible future selves. The existence of models which can represent images of their future selves provides a basis for affiliation. One of the suggested contributors to male marginalization, therefore, is the absence of appropriate role models for boys. It is thus instructive that Thompson (2009) found a correlation of .680 correlation between the variables "my principal shows interest in my concerns" and "I respect my principal".

Ouchi (1981) and Farkas and De Backer (1996) have shown that workers in industry measure the value of the leadership received with reference to the extent to which their leaders show concern for their welfare. I have established that students' respect for principals is related to principals' display of interest in the concerns of students. The results of my study show that the single largest factor responsible for the behaviour of the data is *modelling*, which alone accounted for in excess of 38 per cent of the variation in the data. Modelling has to do with the display of behaviours deemed to be consistent with the values of the society or group of which one is a part and has been found to be related to *accountability* and *respect*. The importance of the demonstration of interest in the concerns of students, therefore, goes to the heart of what it means to be a model and arises from the fact that the society into which students are being sent as products of the education system is characterized by features such as otherness, strangeness, diversity, ambiguity, complexity and plurality, thereby requiring of them the display of such behaviours that will serve the welfare of the society.

One of the inhibitors to the demonstration of concern is dogmatism which is born of a fundamentalist world view which regards the self as the centre and makes all others peripheral. This outlook manifests itself in a refusal to be accountable to others, especially if they are different – different class, gender, power level or educational level. A fundamentalist world view is characterized by the desire for sameness not otherness, familiarity not strangeness and prefabricated responses that are born of uncritical certitude, and which claim authority on all issues rather than a willingness to explore new approaches. An over-reliance on prefabricated answers is born of the notion that there are established and knowable right ways for doing everything.

Students, therefore, who are schooled under fundamentalist oriented leadership do not develop their capacities to listen and show concern. This fundamentalist orientation results in large measure from the thinking that what there is to be known does not reside in otherness, strangeness or diversity. The upshot of this fundamentalist orientation is that students enter a world that is crafted on diversity, characterized by ambiguity, propelled by plurality and steeped in complexity with an orientation of prefabricated postulations which are often out of sync with the realities around them.

Educational leaders model respect in a number of ways: these include listening to others' points of views and stories and learning from them. This disposition builds tolerance for otherness and contribute to the creation of a new framework for supporting students' self-understanding.

Underperformance among students, like underperformance among employees, results from a number of factors, including perceptions of favouritism, inequity, lack of clarity about performance standards and expectations/or confused signals, and weaknesses or deficiencies in relationships, as suggested by Almansour (2012).

I suggest that one of the philosophical orientations of the effective educational leader is the conviction that every student can succeed, that everyone has the capacity to do well (Thompson 2015). Proposition MRM also recognizes that there are often "performance blockers" which stand in the way of members of the team achieving and delivering high levels of performance. Given these twin starting points, transformational leaders invest appropriate energy in looking out for slow learners, below-par performance and disenchanted members of the team who were once at a high level of output but who have fallen behind. It is one of the hallmarks of the transformational leader that they are able to move a self-doubting and low-performing team member or a disgruntled and disillusioned team member to achieve peak performance.

Ouchi's Theory Z was premised on his finding that one of the distinctive features of Japanese versus American leadership was the concern shown by Japanese managers for the welfare of subordinates. Using this reference point, I examined whether students placed value, and if so how much, on the display of concern by their leaders (principals) for students who were faced with challenges of underperformance.

However, the task of transformational classroom leadership is a subset of a larger agenda of managing the learning and student development process so that students are readied for the world into which they are being sent. This task calls for a sharing of roles and responsibilities among classroom teacher, the principal and students. The principal provides leadership for this overall process undertaking a number of tasks according to Leithwood et al. (2004), Poplin (1992) and others. These include:

- Visiting each classroom every day; assisting in some classrooms where the opportunity arises (from time to time) and encouraging teachers to visit one another's classes.
- Involving the whole staff in deliberating on school goals, beliefs and visions at the beginning of the year.
- Helping teachers work smarter by actively seeking different interpretations and checking out assumptions; placing individual problems in

the larger perspective of the whole school; avoiding commitment to preconceived solutions; clarifying and summarizing at key points during meetings; and keeping the group on task, but not imposing your own perspective.
- Using action research teams or school improvement teams as a way of sharing power. Giving everyone responsibilities and involving staff in governance functions. For those not participating, asking them to be in charge of a task group with defined deliverables and timelines.
- Finding the good things that are happening and publicly recognizing the work of staff and students who have contributed to school improvement. Sending private notes to teachers expressing appreciation for special efforts.
- Surveying the staff often about their wants and needs. Being receptive to teachers' attitudes and philosophies. Using active listening and show people you truly care about them.
- Letting teachers experiment with new ideas. Sharing and discussing research with them. Proposing questions for people to think about and decriminalize errors in the search for solutions.
- Using available mechanisms to support teachers, such as finding money for a project or providing time for collaborative planning during the workday. Protecting teachers from the problems of limited time, excessive paperwork and demands from other agencies.
- Letting teachers know they are responsible for all students, not just their own classes.

Educational Supervision and the Realities of the Caribbean

In order to appreciate and provide a more comprehensive assessment of the transformations being pursued in education, and in particular with reference to the Jamaican education system, the current discussions need to be positioned in their wider global context. Governance systems globally are moving towards greater decentralization with increased emphasis on local responsibility, autonomy and accountability. These shifts are also taking place in education. Speaking on global changes that have been affecting schools and the need to adapt internal and regulatory systems to be more in sync with the demands of the current era, Foster (2004) advocates the development of "local" leadership. He lamented the fact that the school's role in developing a democratic polity was being eroded by the existence of excessive rules and regulations. Foster (2004) therefore, emphasized the need for the local school community to have a larger and more significant involvement in its own operations.

Beck (1993) argues for what he calls a more democratic and dialogical approach to teaching and learning. The implications of these developments mean that the resources made available to the school should be increasingly defined by the needs dictated by the collective wisdom and expectation of the local (Foster 2004) community and less and less by the dictates and preconceptions of a sometimes-distant policy centre. It is, therefore, of significance that in the transformation of the education sector in Jamaica the intent is to place greater responsibility and power at the regional (local) level in the regional educational entities with the centre focusing on policy formulation, policy implementation, policy-compliance monitoring and resource allocation. Of course, it is expected that the policy-driven processes of the *centre* will be informed by the needs and realities of the *local* – that is, regional educational entities.

The primary ramification of the foregoing is that the ownership of management responsibilities at the local level – that is, the operations of each school plant, by virtue of being more diverse, will require that external people offering assistance must be far more *au fait* with the tools of diagnosis and intervention and must be able to skilfully take account of the agenda of multiple stakeholders.

Given the demands and expectations of users of educational services on the one hand and the defined policy and operational directions of the Ministry of Education on the other, the question of how the education supervision function should be organized and delivered becomes an important question. A key question is this: *If responsibility is localized as it is proposed and ought to be, and if decision making at the local level should be consultative and inclusive as the demands and expectations of members of the community indicate, how should the education supervision function be understood?*

According to Foster (2004), schools exist to develop virtuous citizens who care about their children and the environment in which they are raised. Among the elements of Jamaica's Vision 2030 are the following:

- That the student becomes a productive citizen-worker in charge of their personal economic advancement
- That students contribute to national development by being

   1. Socially aware and responsible
   2. Conscious of what is good for society
   3. Committed to a sustainable lifestyle
   4. Spiritually conscious and mature
   5. Tolerant of diversity
   6. Rooted in their Jamaican "smaddiness" (personality)

School supervision requires that the supervisor brings to the task a certain degree of knowledge, skill and moral reasoning to help to determine how effective the behaviour of faculty, parents and the community is, in contributing towards the goal of creating a community of virtuous citizens who are productive and contributing to national development. This task requires that the supervisor engages in empowerment activities. To do so, the supervisor must move beyond the traditional notion of supervision in a way that discards the idea of "subordinates" or the "novice" and instead create a culture of collaboration and a community of practice that embraces diversity through the pursuit of both individual and collective goals.

The supervisor, in this mode of thinking, is focused on adding value. Value-added supervision/leadership includes, but is not limited to, providing an epistemological perspective on how problems may be understood; demonstrating how participation may be used advantageously to advance the larger agenda; supporting the integration of diverse skills while emphasizing the importance of being embracive of diversity; focusing the learning process not only on what students learn but who they become; translating the commoditized products of information into prisms of insight to create actions that reflect creativity, originality and innovation; and facilitating avenues for members of the learning community to experience connectedness.

School Supervision as Management Consulting: An Emerging Caribbean Paradigm?

Management consulting as a distinct area of business activity has grown in scope and scale during the last decade and is recognized as one of the most critical sectors in the economic change towards a service and knowledge economy. It continues to be one of the fastest growing sectors. Increasingly businesses, public sector organizations and departments of government and not-for-profit organizations seek the services of management consultants to advise them on a wide range and number of challenges that they confront.

Management consulting involves the use of specialist skills to inform the provision of objective advice based on the analysis of data and information with the aim of creating value, maximizing growth or improving the business performance of the consultant's clients. Management consultants are primarily concerned with the strategy, structure, management processes and operations of an organization and seek to assist clients (invariably organizations) by detecting and defining problems, identifying options and recommending solutions. Management consultants may also provide additional resources and/or assist in the implementation of solutions.

Consultants operate across a wide variety of services such as business strategy, marketing, financial and management controls, human resources, information technology, e-business and operations and supply-chain management. Every industry employs the services of management consultants. As with the type of work, the range of consultancy firms also varies from the larger firms that offer end-to-end solutions to smaller or niche firms that offer specialist expertise, skills and industry knowledge.

The required elements in the consultant's body of knowledge are:

- strategic management
- financial management
- human resources management
- information technology management
- marketing management
- operations management

The management consultancy concept as it would apply to schools would require a consultant to have core and specialist knowledge in at least one field (e.g., educational administration, curriculum development, finance, marketing and engineering). However, it is not the possession of knowledge in the specialist area that "makes one a consultant" rather it is the ability to apply that knowledge in helping the client to address issues that may be related to any or all of the areas in the consultant's body of knowledge and to do so with due regard for the canons of professional ethics. Thus, a management consultant is known for their capacity to help a client identify systemic blockages to organizational excellence and provide the "how to" advice to overcome those blockages. A simplified description of the modus operandi, or characteristics, of the management consultant is as follows:

- Help clients to assess their business situation, challenges and opportunities.
- Help clients to develop strategies for improvement.
- Helps clients to develop an action plan.
- Helps clients to secure resources.
- Builds client capability.
- Conforms to the code of ethics.

The Education Officer as a Management Consultant

The work that an education officer would do is consistent with the functions performed by a management consultant is shown in table 6.1. When closely examined, it will be seen that the functions that management consultants perform are identical in nature, even though they may differ in scope and emphasis from the work performed by education officers. It is my assertion that the consultative, inclusionary nature of the mode of operation of the management consultant renders that function inherently transformational. The normal terms of reference of most management consulting assignments is that of enabling the business to improve in one way or the other. Looked at through the TQM prism of continuous improvement, management consulting is, at its core, a TQM-oriented activity. By extension, therefore, education supervision, which depends for its effectiveness on consultation and inclusiveness in order to arrive at solutions for quality improvements, is at its best when it assumes a management consulting approach which involves and requires a transformational leadership direction of engagement.

Table 6.1. Alignment of (Some) Education Officers' Functions with Characteristics of Management Consulting

Functions of Education Officers	Characteristics of Management Consulting
Creates a system-wide mindset for school improvement by incorporating action research to instil a professional problem-solving ethos in the school	Helps clients to assess their business situation, challenges and opportunities
Insures that curriculum planning leads to successful curriculum implementation by being knowledgeable of school improvement and change process	Helps clients to develop strategies for improvement
Knows, understands and adheres to the code of ethics	Conforms to the code of ethics
Identifies specific goals, objectives and evaluation standards that will guide programme evaluation efforts by involving key stakeholders in the evaluation effort	Helps clients to develop an action plan
Examines that school leaders provide governance and leadership that promotes student performance and school effectiveness	Builds client capability
Assists principals to systematize their decision making, problem solving, implementation actions and progress monitoring for making all aspects of the educational enterprise more inclusive of and responsive to social diversity	Helps clients secure resources

In carrying out the task of school supervision, the education officer would explore school performance using a number of metrics and thereby would examine a variety of issues. In appendix section B, I share an instrument I developed and have used in my work with a number of tertiary institutions and which the Ministry of Education had determined should be adopted and used at the secondary level.

Pradhan (2011) asserts that the value of hiring a management consultant lies broadly in the fact that they bring superior analytical skills to the context, based on their knowledge of industry practices. An education officer is expected to possess superior analytical skills and be exposed to various industry practices and thus be able to help a client (school) examine their existing practices within the context of industry best practices.

The school is an organization. Each school is distinctly different. Each has its own peculiar history, elements of process, leadership practices, culture, resources and community support, and so on. The role of the education officer is that of helping a school to make sense of its internal and external contextual realities as it plans performance improvements at all levels. In more specific terms, the role of the education officer is to

- help the school assess its environment, including the social milieu of its customers and publics, its challenges and opportunities;
- help the leadership develop strategies for improving student outcomes through improvement in the management of resources, systems of accountability, staff morale and organizational efficiency;
- help the school to move (within acceptable time frames and within budget) from planning to implementation;
- help the school undertake effective human resource development programmes and establish succession planning process;
- help the school secure resources;
- conduct all of the above with a keen eye for issues such as conflicts of interest, stakeholder relations and professional conduct;
- help the school in its day-to-day operations and to remain in compliance with all relevant standards, codes and regulations applicable to the education and care of minors and for ensuring their healthy development; and
- help the school to observe the appropriate protocols for the employment, remuneration and conduct of employed staff.

The kernel of the tasks described above constitutes the functions performed by management and, as such, the business of school supervision is in fact a form of management consulting. By developing the perspective that education officers/ supervisors are in fact performing the role of management consultants and by instilling this notion into the education community and its language and culture, a number of outcomes are inevitable, chief of which are

1. locating responsibility and accountability where they properly belong – with the leadership of the school;
2. a sharper sense of obligation on the part of the education officer to ensure that they deliver/add value to the school both by the analyses conducted and the recommendations and support offered;
3. the strengthening of the facilitator role rather than that of supervisor (which a management consultant is not);
4. the emergence of greater levels of professional independent judgement that is evidence based, well documented and open to scrutiny;
5. greater focus on the strengthening of the capacities of others and less attention to the notion of the education officer as invested with all expert knowledge;
6. the creation of a more thorough-going atmosphere of support but also adequate distance to allow for meaningful evaluation, non-threatening conversations about performance and objective measurement of outcomes;
7. self-evaluation by the leadership in an environment of accountability; and
8. collective responsibility for outcomes at the local level.

7 | A Concluding Word: Claiming a New Paradigm for Educational Leadership in the Caribbean

The basic argument of this book is that educational leadership in the Caribbean a postmodern era requires reimagination. This reimagination has to be informed by an approach of radical inclusivity and power sharing. This approach is predicated on the assumption that students are capable of offering meaningful suggestions for improvements in the processes of teaching and delivery of learning, and practitioners possess knowledge and experience that must be used to inform policy. At the heart of this proposed new approach to educational leadership is the contention that zones of exclusive expertise have been overturned by the advent of postmodernism which, among other things, is characterized by the challenging of convention, the embrace of otherness, the diversification of authority and the commoditization of knowledge. In this regard, the focus of assessments of the usefulness of ideas should not be on whose ideas they are or the "pedigree" of the one making the suggestion; rather, the focus should be on the merits of the idea, regardless of source.

The openness to new ideas as a focus of educational leadership in a postmodern era does not assume a naivety that assumes that ideas are ideologically or politically neutral and thus should not be approached with a level of scepticism. On the contrary, the proposed agenda of openness that this book advances is premised on the notion that all ideas are ideologically and politically coloured – whether incipiently, unconsciously or consciously. For this reason, all suggestions and ideas should be approached with a healthy sense of criticism, including self-criticism, and put to the utmost test of validity and objectivity before being accepted and implemented. But given that at any given point in the process of teaching and learning or the making of policy, there are precedents, existing practices and established policy, the approach to engaging new ideas should begin with the recognition that what is can be improved upon even while being practised or tested.

This book also advances the view that educational leadership in a postmodern era demands of educational leaders in the Caribbean a new look at issues such as the role of TVET in the general curriculum within a context of inclusive and SD. The premises of this assertion include a the contention that TVET offers ways of learning that are akin to the characteristics of postmodernism and Proposition MRM. This position contends that TVET allows students more room for deep involvement in learning, facilitates the acquisition of life skills and fosters greater personal independence, thus creating the foundations for SD. These ideas are akin to Proposition MRM, which, among other things, promotes inclusivity, shared responsibility, mutual respect, critical thinking and solutions-focused learning, all of which are critical elements of SD. Thus, this book makes the claim that, on the one hand, Proposition MRM and the essential spirit of postmodernism are kindred souls while, on the other, accepting the view that TVET and SD represent the sides of the same coin.

This book also advances the view that a consulting approach ought to characterize the relationship between the education officer and principal at the intersection where educational policy and practice meet. Specifically, the view advanced in this book is that education officers should seek to facilitate discursive engagement in the supervisory process when the policy imperatives of the ministry are being transmitted for practise and application at the school level. Underlying this perspective is that view that there is a duty to reckon that in a postmodern era, in which great ideas come from multiple places and there are many possible paths to truths, the relationship between the education officer and principal should be like that of a management consultant with a client. This management consultant–client relationship places the education officer in the role of observer, critic, adviser, evaluator, supporter and chief improvement officer, not lord or dictator. These functions are consistent with the characteristics of postmodernism and Proposition MRM.

Afterword

PAULA SHAW

"That postmodernism affirms that every point of view is open to critique does not represent pessimism, rather it is a form of bold optimism and faith in the belief that the shapers of human society and its institutions can always improve and find better and more effective and relevant ways of dealing with the issues confronting them." So says Thompson in the very first chapter of his book. Not only does this thought encapsulate, in large part, the essence of his book but it acts as a guiding light for the author's discussion regarding the issues, applications and views which are expressed throughout its pages. The main ideas regarding educational leadership are Thompson's focus and subsequent to his thorough dissection, we are not disappointed by the careful reconstruction of his fresh views on educational leadership.

The text offers new insight to its readers, chiefly those who lead organizations, particularly educational institutions, yet it does not exclude classroom teachers or other teaching professionals. Those who study the philosophy of the structure of educational institutions and those who seek to set education policy at the local and national level would also benefit from what he has to say.

This book begins with a discussion of the history of the postmodern era; to those who have never had reason to think about postmodernism, the discourse is an education. To those who are familiar with the concept the discussion elucidates the debate as to the effect of postmodernism as a phenomenon and its iterative relationship with other twenty-first century world views. Thompson explores the implications for the adoption of the philosophy behind postmodernism;

intermingled in the discussion are his ideas on the relevance of postmodernism to the growth and development of institutions within society in general and within Caribbean society in particular. Thompson answers the questions of those who seek to understand why an appreciation of the postmodern era is important, even though it is still unfolding. His arguments are compelling more so because they are grounded, within his local research and experience and yet not to the exclusion of a deference to international research.

As in his previous works, Thompson looks at leadership not only as it applies to education but as it is couched within wider organizational theory and management research. This broad approach is justified if one appreciates the ability of leadership to transform organizations and the people who give them energy and their *raison d'être*. For those who are missing the key to success within the sphere of business, the ideas expressed in chapter 2 are food for thought. For those who hold leadership positions within educational institutions or who are involved in teaching and learning, the author asserts proposition modelling, respect, motivation.

Proposition MRM is an evidence-based theory which recommends itself for application to the positive growth of the practice of all educators and which has special significance for those who form the leadership of educational institutions. An acronym for modelling, respect and motivation Thompson's Proposition MRM highlights the critical qualities of and for educational leadership in the postmodern era. At a fundamental level, the tenets of Proposition MRM can be used as a guide for interactions between teachers and their students and also among a faculty of teachers. In fact, all stakeholders within institutions of learning would do well to consider the adoption of proposition.

Further, Thompson submits Proposition MRM as an intriguing lens through which to view educational leadership. It represents a model of critical thinking regarding collaborative leadership; it reflects how the diverse expectations of those who are led can be effectively harnessed by a power-sharing approach by those who lead.

In chapters 4 and 5, Thompson makes the real-world connections alluded to in the opening chapters, linking Proposition MRM and postmodernism and making a strong argument for the importance of TVET in mainstream education. He also uses this connectivity to make a case for encouraging the sustainable development of natural, social and economic resources within the Caribbean Community. Within the realm of national education policy, one of the tools the author promotes is an advancement of the role of the education officer to one more akin to that of management consultant and he sets out the far-reaching possibilities of such a paradigm shift in thinking.

The inclusion of the philosophies of Caribbean thinkers Manley, Nettleford and Ramphal grounds the discussion of the postmodern approach within the local context and represents the importance of "defining our own epistemologies [and] developing our own theories" (Thompson 2017). As the philosophy of postmodernism suggests, there is no one truth and so the discussions and topics explored in the book are wide-ranging. Yet within its extensiveness, the peculiarities of our experience in Jamaica and the Caribbean are given the required emphasis, on par with those once proclaimed "divine truths" in a Eurocentric world. It is Thompson's exploration of the intersection of ideas like Proposition MRM and TVET coupled with an attempt to see how some or all of these could be applied to sustainable development in the economy which heightens the perceptive content of the work.

Thompson's detailed exploration of the concepts of postmodernism and educational leadership, plus the evolution of management theory, offers important references to all who consider that they are students of the theory of administration and educational leadership. This book not only gives a historical perspective of these areas but also demonstrates how with keen intellectual application the knowledge gained from unpacking concepts and then realigning and re-forming the key ideas gleaned from the process, new connectivities can to be found. Thompson's strategy creates an interconnectedness among the concepts he has brought to the fore with creativity, originality and innovation.

Appendix

Students' Questionnaire: Students' Perceptions and Expectations of Leadership in a Postmodern Era

Dear Friend, Thanks for your willingness to take part in this survey. Your school has been selected because I believe you can help me get a better understanding of a number of things about which students are concerned. Thanks for taking the time to answer all questions as honestly and completely as you can. There is no right or wrong answer. It will take you about 15 minutes to complete to answer all questions. Simply tick the response that you think best reflects your views and experiences. Thanks again.

SECTION A: DEMOGRAPHICS

1. Gender:	(a) Male	[ ]	(b) Female	[ ]
2. Form:	(a) 4th	[ ]	(b) 5th	[ ]
3. Location of School:	(a) Urban	[ ]	(b) Rural	[ ]
4. Type of School:	(a) Traditional High	[ ]	(b) New Sec	[ ]

SECTION B: The Following Statements Are about Your Views and Experiences in Your Relationship with Your Teacher

	Strongly Agree	Agree	Unsure	Disagree	Strongly Disagree
1. My teacher shows interest in my opinions					
2. My teachers encourage students to hold points of views that may differ from his or her own					
3. My teacher responds positively when students disagree with him or her					
4. My teacher does not try to dictate what students should think					
5. I respect my teacher					
6. My teacher's teaching style contributes to my level of motivation					
7. My academic performance is influenced by my teacher's style of teaching					
8. I feel respected by my teacher					
9. I feel that my teacher makes an effort to make school work exciting					
10. I have a close relationship with my teacher					
11. My attitude towards others is influenced by my relationship with my teacher					
12. I believe I am being adequately prepared for life after school					
13. I am often commended by my teacher					
14. I listen to my teacher's advice					
15. I am a highly motivated student					

SECTION C: The Following Statements Relate to Your Subject Teacher

	Strongly Agree	Agree	Unsure	Disagree	Strongly Disagree
1. My teacher accepts that he or she is not always right in how an issue may viewed					
2. My teacher conveys to students that there may be more than one correct approach to a given situation					
3. My teacher knows his or her subject matter very well					
4. My teacher is a good role model					
5. My teacher encourages me to have confidence in myself					
6. My teacher likes to engage in debates with students					
7. My teacher is a good listener					
8. My teacher accepts correction from students					
9. My teacher makes learning applicable to real life issues					
10. My teacher encourages students to be tolerant of differing points of view					

SECTION D: The Following Statements Are about Your School and Principal

	Strongly Agree	Agree	Unsure	Disagree	Strongly Disagree
1. At my school there is a strong emphasis on academic performance					
2. At my school students are encouraged to develop and express their own points of views					
3. At my school teachers believe they can learn from students					

(Section D continues)

SECTION D: The Following Statements Are about Your School and Principal *(continued)*

	Strongly Agree	Agree	Unsure	Disagree	Strongly Disagree
4. At my school it is viewed as a good thing when students try to get answers from teachers on the reasons for some of their decisions					
5. My principal takes a positive interest in students who are not performing to their best					
6. My principal takes an interest in the concerns of students					
7. My principal takes the views of students into consideration before making some decisions					
8. My principal shows respect to students					
9. I respect my principal					
10. My principal is a good role model					
11. My principal is a good leader					
12. My principal is a good listener					
13. My principal behaves as if he or she owns the school					
14. My principal encourages students to be critical thinkers					
15. I would feel comfortable expressing my opinions to my principal if I disagreed with something					

References

Allport, Gordon W. 1937. "The Functional Autonomy of Motives". *American Journal of Psychology* 50:141–56.
Almansour, Y.M. 2012. "The Relationship between Leadership Styles and Motivation of Managers Conceptual Framework". *Journal of Arts, Science and Commerce* 3, no. 1: 161–66.
Anderson, P. 1998. *The Origins of Postmodernity.* London: Verso.
Baghramian, Maria, and Carter, J. Adam. 2015. "Relativism". *PhilPapers.* https://philpapers.org/rec/BAGR-6.
Bagnall, R.G. 1994. "Continuing Education in Postmodernity". *International Journal of Lifelong Education* 13, no. 14: 265–79.
Barnard, C. 1938. *The Functions of the Executive.* Cambridge: Harvard University Press.
Barton, D., A. Grant and M. Horn. 2012. "Leading in the 21st Century". *McKinsey Quarterly* 3:30–47.
Batista-Taran, L.C., M.B. Shuck, C.C. Gutierrez and S. Baralt. 2009. "The Role of Leadership Style in Employee Engagement". In *Proceedings of the Eighth Annual College of Education and GSN Research Conference,* edited by M.S. Plakhotnik, S.M. Nielsen and D.M. Pane, 15–20. Miami: Florida International University.
Bauman, Z., and K. Tester. 2007. "On the Postmodernism Debate". In *Postmodernism. What Moment?*, edited by P. Goulimari, 22–31. Manchester: Manchester University Press.
Beck, C. 1993. *Postmodernism, Pedagogy and the Philosophy of Education.* http://www.ed.uiuc.edu.
Beckett, L., R.D. Glass and A.P. Moreno. 2013. "A Pedagogy of Community Building: Re-imagining Parent Involvement and Community Organizing in Popular Education Efforts". *Association of Mexican American Educators Journal* 6, no. 1: 5–14.
Berger, P.L., and T. Luckman. 1967. *The Social Construction of Reality.* Garden City: Anchor.
Berkeley, B. 2012. "The Relevance of Postmodern Epistemologies in Multicultural Studies in the Caribbean". *Journal of the Department of Behavioural Sciences* 1, no. 1: 118–23.
Billett, S. 2013. "Learning through Practice: Beyond Informal and towards a Framework for Learning through Practice". In *Revisiting Global Trends in TVET: Reflections on Theory and Practice,* 123–63. Bonn: UNESCO-UNEVOC.

Blake, R.R., and J.S. Mouton. 1994. *The Managerial Grid: Leadership Styles for Achieving Production through People.* Houston: Gulf Publishing.

Boodhai, N. N.d. "Concept Paper for the Development of a CARICOM Strategic Plan for Vocational Education Services in the CARICOM Single Market and Economy (CSME)". Paper prepared for the Arthur Lok Jack School of Business, University of the West Indies, St Augustine, Trinidad and Tobago. http://www.csmeonline.org/news/documents/research/services-research/22-concept-paper-vocational-eduction/file.

Bozalek, V., and M. Zembylas. 2017. "Towards a Response-able Pedagogy across Higher Education Institutions in Post-Apartheid South Africa: An Ethico-Political Analysis". *Education as Change* 21, no. 2: 62–85.

Briton, D. 1996. *The Modern Practice of Adult Education: A Post-modern Critique.* New York: SUNY Press.

Brown, S., and P. Bryant. 2015. "Getting to Know the Elephant: A Call to Advance Servant Leadership through Construct Consensus, Empirical Evidence, and Multilevel Theoretical Development". *Servant Leadership: Theory and Practice* 2, no. 1: 10–35.

Burkus, D. 2013. "How Criticism Creates Innovative Teams". *Harvard Business Review*, 22 July.

Campion, M.A., E.M. Papper and G.J. Medsker. 1996. "Relations between Work Team Characteristics and Effectiveness: A Replication and Extension". *Personnel Psychology* 49, no. 2: 429–452.

Carson, D.A. 1996. *The Gagging of God: Christianity Confronts Pluralism.* Grand Rapids: Zondervan Publishing House.

Conley, D.T., and P. Goldman. 1994. "Ten Propositions for Facilitative Leadership". In *Reshaping the Principalship: Insights from Transformational Reform Efforts*, edited by J. Murphy and K.S. Louis, 237–62. Thousand Oaks, CA: Corwin.

Coopey, J. 1995. "The Learning Organization – Power, Politics, and Ideology". In *Management Learning.* Thousand Oaks, CA: Sage.

Cusimano, J. 1996. "Managers as Facilitators". *Training and Development,* September.

Dambe, M., and F. Moorad. 2008. "From Power to Empowerment: A Paradigm Shift in Leadership". *South African Journal of Higher Education* 22, no. 3: 575–87.

Durkheim, E. 1979. *The Elementary Forms of the Religious Life.* New York: Free Press.

Eccles, J.S., A. Wigfield and U. Schiefele. 1998. "Motivation to Succeed." In *Handbook of Child Psychology: Social, Emotional, and Personality Development*, edited by W. Damon and N. Eisenberg, 1017–95. Hoboken, NJ: Wiley.

Edwards, R., and R. Usher. 1995. "Postmodernity and the Educating of Educators". In *The Canmore Proceedings*, edited by M. Collin, 109–16. Saskatoon: University of Saskatchewan.

Farkas, C.M., and S. Wetlaufer. 1996. "The Ways Chief Executive Officers Lead". *Harvard Business Review* 74, no. 3 (May–June): 110.

Fayol, H. 1949. *General and Industrial Administration.* New York: Pitman.

Foster, W.P. 2004. "The Decline of the Local: A Challenge to Educational Leadership". *Educational Administration Quarterly* 40, no. 2: 176–91.

Fowler, J.W. 1996. *Faithful Change: The Personal and Public Challenges of Postmodern Life.* Nashville: Abingdon Press.

Freire, P. 1970. *Pedagogy of the Oppressed*. New York: Continuum.
Garratt, B. 1987. *The Learning Organization*. London: Fontana.
Geofroy, S. 2007. "Freedom, Post-modernism, and Caribbean Masculine 'Re-descriptions' Jouissance/Postcolonial Dislocation".
Glanz, J., and R.F. Neville. 1997. *Educational Supervision: Perspectives, Issues and Controversies*. Norwood, MA: Christopher-Gordon.
Goleman, D. 1998. *Working with Emotional Intelligence*. New York: Bantam Books.
Gordon, S.P., and M. Reese. 1997. "High-Stakes Testing: Worth the Price?". *Journal of School Leadership* 7:345–68.
Greenleaf, R.K. 1970/2002. "The Servant as Leader". In *Servant Leadership: A Journey into the Nature of Legitimate Power and Greatness*, edited by L.C. Spears and Robert K. Greenleaf, 21–61. Mahwah: Paulist Press.
Grenz, S. 1996. *A Primer on Postmodernism*. Grand Rapids, MI: Eerdmans.
Grogan, M. 2004. "Keeping a Critical, Postmodern Eye on Educational Leadership in the United States: In Appreciation of Bill Foster". *Educational Administration Quarterly* 40, no. 2: 222–39.
Growe, R. 2011. "Collaborative Leadership in the Era of New Normal". *National Forum of Educational Administration and Supervision Journal* 29, no. 4: 1–6.
Gulick, L., and L. Urwick, eds. 1937. *Papers on the Science of Administration*. New York: Institute of Public Administration.
Guo, Z., and S. Lamb. 2010. *International Comparisons of China's Technical and Vocational Education and Training System*. Dordrecht, Netherlands: Springer.
Hallinger, P. 1992. "The Evolving Role of American Principals: From Managerial to Instructional to Transformational Leaders". *Journal of Educational Administration* 30, no. 3: 35–48.
Hallinger, P., and R. Heck. 1996. "Reassessing the Principal's Role in School Effectiveness: A Review of Empirical Research 1980–1995". *Educational Administration Quarterly* 32:5–44.
Hamidifar, F. 2010. "A Study of the Relationship between Leadership Styles and Employee Job Satisfaction at IAU in Tehran, Iran". *Au-GSB e-Journal* 3, no. 1.
Harter, J.K., F.L. Schmidt and T.L. Hayes. 2002. "Business-Unit-Level Relationship between Employee Satisfaction, Employee Engagement, and Business Outcomes: A Meta-analysis". *Journal of Applied Psychology* 87, no. 2: 268.
Harvey, D. 1990. *The Condition of Postmodernity: An Enquiry into the Origins of Cultural Change*. Oxford: Blackwell.
Hecht, B. 2013. "Why Collaboration Is the New Competition". *Harvard Business Review* 10. https://hbr.org/2013/01/collaboration-is-the-new-compe.
Heck, R., G.A. Marcoulides and P. Lang. 1991. "Principal Instructional Leadership and School Achievement: The Application of Discriminant Techniques". *School Effectiveness and School Improvement* 2, no. 2: 115–35.
Hersey, P., and K.H. Blanchard. 1982. Leadership Style: Attitudes and Behaviors. *Training and Development Journal* 36, no. 5: 50–52.
Herzberg, F.I. 1966. *Work and the Nature of Man*. Oxford: World Publishing.
Higman, B.W. 2008. *Plantation Jamaica, 1750–1850: Capital and Control in a Colonial Economy*. Kingston: University of the West Indies Press.

Hoy, W.K., and C.G. Miskel. 1996. *Educational Administration: Theory, Research, and Practice*. New York, NY: McGraw-Hill.

Hughes, J., and O.M. Kwok. 2007. "Influence of Student-Teacher and Parent-Teacher Relationships on Lower Achieving Readers' Engagement and Achievement in the Primary Grades". *Journal of Educational Psychology* 99, no. 1: 39.

Hutton, D. 2009. "Preparing the Workforce for the 21st Century: The Jamaican Experience". *Caribbean Journal of Education* 31, no. 1: 21–45.

Illich, I. 1970. *Deschooling Society*. New York: Harper and Row

Johnson, P., and J. Duberley. 2000. *Understanding Management Research: An Introduction to Epistemology*. Thousand Oaks, CA: Sage. http://dx.doi.org/10.4135/9780857020185.

Jules, D. 2012. *Promoting the Attractiveness of TVET in the Context of Secondary Education Reform*. https://www.cxc.org/annual-reports/2012/assets/Promoting_the_Attractiveness_of_TVET.pdf.

Kahn, W.A. 1990. "Psychological Conditions of Personal Engagement and Disengagement at Work". *Academy of Management Journal* 33, no. 4: 692–724.

Kaye, B., and B. Jacobson. 1996. "Reframing Mentoring". *Training and Development* 50, no. 8: 44–47.

Keunzli-Monard, F., and A. Keunzli. 2004. *Postmodernism Compared with Existential Bases Therapies (Gestalt): Food for Conversations*. http://www.hal-pc.org/~boha/pmg.htm.

KhosraviShakib, M. 2010. "Marxist Feminism and Postmodernism". *Journal of Languages and Culture* 1, no. 3: 28–34.

Knitter, P.F. 1985. *No Other Name?: A Critical Survey of Christian Attitudes toward the World Religions*. Vol. 7. New York: Orbis Books.

Kocolowski, M.D. 2010. "Shared Leadership: Is It Time for a Change". *Emerging Leadership Journeys* 3, no. 1: 22–32.

Labelle, R. 2005. *ICT Policy Formulation and e-Strategy Development: A Comprehensive Guidebook*. New Delhi: Elsevier.

Lai, E.R. 2011. "Critical Thinking: A Literature Review". *Pearson's Research Reports* 6:40–41.

Leithwood, K., K.S. Louis, S. Anderson and K. Wahlstrom. 2004. *How Leadership Influences Student Learning*. New York: The Wallace Foundation.

Likert, R. 1987. *New Patterns of Management*. New York: Garland.

Lloyd, M., and N. Bahr. 2010. "Thinking Critically about Critical Thinking in Higher Education". *International Journal for the Scholarship of Teaching and Learning* 4, no. 2: Article 9.

Lyotard, J.F. 1979. *The Postmodern Condition: A Report on Knowledge*. Manchester: Manchester University Press.

———. 1999. "The Postmodern Condition". *Modernity: Critical Concepts* 4:161–77.

Manley, M. 1975. *A Voice at the Workplace; Reflections on Colonialism and the Jamaican Worker*. London: Deutsch.

———. 1987. *Up the Down Escalator: Development and the International Economy – A Jamaican Case Study*. Washington: Howard University Press.

Maslow, A. 1970. *Motivation and Personality*. Reading: Addison-Wesley.

Mayo, E. 1933. *The Human Problems of an Industrial Civilization*. New York: Macmillan.

McCullum, D. N.d. "Comparing Modernist and Postmodern Educational Theory". https://www.xenos.org/essays/comparing-modernist-and-postmodern-educational-theory.
McGregor, D. 1960. "Theory X and Theory Y". *Organization Theory* 358:374.
Mead, G. 1934. *Mind, Self and Society*. Chicago: University of Chicago Press.
Miller, E.L. 1984. *Educational Research: The English-Speaking Caribbean*. Ottawa, ON: The International Development Research Centre.
Miller, E.L. 1989. *Gender Composition of the Primary School Teaching Force: A Result of Personal Choice?* Women and Development Studies, Faculty of Education and the Women's Studies Group, University of the West Indies.
Morris, H.A. 2009. "Developing Policies for Technical and Vocational Education Training (TVET) in the Caribbean". *Caribbean Journal of Education* 31, no. 1: 1–20.
Murphy, J. 1990. "Principal Instructional Leadership". *Advances in Educational Administration: Changing Perspectives on the School* 1, Part B: 163–200.
Nettleford, R.M. 1970. *Mirror Mirror: Identify, Race, and Protest in Jamaica*. Kingston: W. Collins and Sangster.
O'Leary, R., and L.B. Bingham, eds. 2009. *The Collaborative Public Manager: New Ideas for the Twenty-First Century*. Washington, DC: Georgetown University Press.
Ouchi, W. 1993. *Theory Z: How American Businesses Can Meet the Japanese Challenge*. New York: Avon Books.
Ouchi, William G. 1981. *Theory Z: How American Businesses Can Meet the Japanese Challenge*. New York: Avon Books.
Padgett, A.G. 1996. "Christianity and Postmodernity". *Christian Scholar's Review* 26, no. 2: 129–32.
Parry, Odette. 2000. *Male Underachievement in High School Education in Jamaica, Barbados, and St Vincent and the Grenadines*. Kingston: Canoe Press.
Pearce, C.L., C.L. Wassenaar and C.C. Manz. 2014. "Is Shared Leadership the Key to Responsible Leadership?". *Academy of Management Perspectives* 28, no. 3: 275–88.
Pedler, M., T. Boydell and J. Burgoyne. 1988. *Learning Company Project Report*. Sheffield: Manpower Services Commission.
Pescuric, A., and W. Byham. 1996. "The New Look at Behaviour Modelling". *Training and Development*, July.
Peters, T. 2010. *The Tom Peters Seminar: Crazy Times Call for Crazy Organizations*. New York: Vintage.
Peters, T., and R.H. Watermann. 1982. *In Search of Excellence*. New York: Harper.
Phillips, A. 2007. *Multiculturalism Without Culture*. Vol. 14. Princeton, NJ: Princeton University Press.
Poplin, M.S. 1992. "The Leader's New Role: Looking to the Growth of Teachers". *Educational Leadership* 49, no. 5: 10–11.
Porath, C. 2015. "The Leadership Behavior That's Most Important to Employees". *Harvard Business Review Blog*. https://hbr.org/2015/05/the-leadership-behavior-thats-most-important-to-employees.
Pradeep, D.D., and N.R.V. Prabhu. 2011. "The Relationship between Effective Leadership and Employee Performance". In *International Conference on Advancements in*

Information Technology with Workshop of ICBMG IPCSIT, Vol. 20. Vol. 207, 198. Singapore: IACSIT Press.

Pradhan, B. 2011. *The Role of Management Consulting.* https://www.enterpriseirregulars.com/33057/the-role-of-management-consulting/.

Ramphall, D. 1997. "Postmodernism and the Rewriting of Caribbean Radical Development Thinking". *Social and Economic Studies* 46, no. 1: 1–30.

Rapley, J. 2004. *Globalization and Inequality: Neoliberalism's Downward Spiral.* London: Lynne Rienner.

Ratnata, I.W. 2013. "Enhancing the Image and Attractiveness of TVET. *TVET@ Asia* 1, no. 1–13. www.tvet-online.asia/issue1/ ratnata_tvet1.pdf.

Robertson, R. 1992. *Globalization: Social Theory and Global Culture,* vol. 16. London: Sage.

Rorty, R. 1985. "Postmodernist Bourgeois Liberalism". In *Hermeneutics and Praxis,* edited by R. Hollinger, 197–202. Notre Dame: University of Notre Dame Press.

Schein, E. 1993. "How Can Organizations Learn Faster? The Challenge of Entering the Green Room". *Sloan Management Review,* Winter.

Senge, P. 1990. *The Fifth Discipline: The Art and Practice of the Learning Organization.* New York: Currency and Doubleday.

Sergiovanni, T.J. 1991. *The Principalship: A Reflective Practice Perspective.* Boston: Allyn and Bacon.

Sexton, T.L. 1997. "Constructivist Thinking within the History of Ideas: The Challenge of a New Paradigm". In *Constructivist Thinking in Counselling Practice, Research, and Training,* edited by T.L. Sexton and B.L. Griffin, 3–18. New York: Teachers College Press.

Shafie, B., S. Baghersalimi, and V. Barghi. 2013. "The Relationship between Leadership Style and Employee Performance". *Singaporean Journal of Business Economics and Management Studies* 2:21–29.

Sheppard, B. 1996. "Exploring the Transformational Nature of Instructional Leadership". *Alberta Journal of Educational Research* 42, no. 4: 325–44.

Simiyu, John W. 2009. *Revitalizing a Technical Training Institute in Kenya: A Case Study of Kaiboi Technical Training Institute, Eldoret, Kenya.* Bonn: UNESCO-UNEVOC.

Simon, H.A. 1957. *Models of Man; Social and Rational.* Oxford: Wiley.

Strock, J.M., and Á. Cabrera. 2010. *Serve to Lead: Your Transformational 21st Century Leadership System.* USA: Serve to Lead Press.

Sweet, R. 2013. "Work-Based Learning: Why? How?". In *Revisiting Global Trends in TVET: Reflections on Theory and Practice.* Bonn: UNESCO-UNEVOC.

Taylor, E.W. 2007. "An Update of Transformative Learning Theory: A Critical Review of the Empirical Research (1999–2005)". *International Journal of Lifelong Education* 26, no. 2: 173–91.

Taylor, F.W. 1911. *The Principles of Scientific Management.* New York: Harper.

Thompson, C.S. 2009. *Towards Solutions: Fundamentals of Transformational Leadership in a Postmodern Era.* Mandeville, Jamaica: NCU Press.

———. 2013. *Leadership Reimagination: A Primer of Principles and Practices.* Kingston: Caribbean Leadership Reimagination Initiative.

———. 2015. *Locating the Epicentre of Effective (Educational) Leadership in the 21st Century.* Kingston: Caribbean Leadership Re-Imagination Initiative.

Tikly, L. 2013. "Reconceptualizing TVET and Development: A Human Capability and Social Justice Approach". In *Revisiting Global Trends in TVET: Reflections on Theory and Practice*, edited by K. Ananiadou. Bonn: UNESCO-UNEVOC.

Tutu, D. 2004. *God Has a Dream: A Vision of Hope for Our Time*. New York: Doubleday.

Ullman, J.L. 1997. "A Case Study of an Urban High School English Class: Encouraging Academic Engagement by Creating a Culture of Respect". Boston College Dissertations and Theses, AAI9813680.

UNESCO. 2005. "Revised Recommendation Concerning Technical and Vocational Education (2001)". In *Normative Instruments Concerning Technical and Vocational Education*. Paris: UNESCO.

———. 2013. *Revisiting Global Trends in TVET: Reflections on Theory and Practice*. Paris: UNESCO.

Usher, R., I. Bryant and R. Johnston. 1997. *Adult Education and the Postmodern Challenge*. London: Routledge.

Vygotsky, L. 1978. "Interaction between Learning and Development". *Readings on the Development of Children* 23, no. 3: 34–41.

Wanzare, Z., and J.L. Da Costa. 2001. "Rethinking Instructional Leadership Roles of the School Principal: Challenges and Prospects". *Journal of Educational Thought/Revue de la Pensée Educative* 35, no. 3: 269–95.

Weber, M. 1947. *The Theory of Economic and Social Organization*. Translated by A.M. Henderson and Talcott Parsons. New York: Oxford University Press.

Winch, C. 2013. "The Attractiveness of TVET". In *Revisiting Global Trends in TVET: Reflections on Theory and Practice*, edited by K. Ananiadou. Bonn: UNESCO-UNEVOC.

Wood, A.W. 1999. *Kant's Ethical Thought*. Cambridge: Cambridge University Press.

Zhang, Y., T.B. Lin and S. Fong Foo. 2012. "Servant Leadership: A Preferred Style of School Leadership in Singapore". *Chinese Management Studies* 6, no. 2: 369–83.

Zhao, Z. 2011. "School-Enterprise Cooperation in China's Vocational Education and Training". In *Assuring the Acquisition of Expertise: Apprenticeship in the Modern Economy*, edited by Z. Zhao, F. Rauner and U. Hauschildt, 43–54. Beijing: Foreign Language Teaching and Research Press.

Index

Act on the Promotion of Industrial Education and Industry-Academy-Research Institute Cooperation, 77
Act on the Promotion of Vocational Education and Training, 77
act utilitarianism, 59–60
adult education, 79
Agenda 21, 72, 73
Age of Enlightenment, 3
age of globalization, 14
Allport, Gordon W, 72
Anderson, P., 13, 20

Baghramian, Maria, 14
Bagnall, R.G., 49
Bailey (1998), 22
Barbados, 3, 22
Barnard, C., 30, 45
Bauman, Z., 20
Beck, C., 38, 91
Beckett, L., 73
behavioural science era, 32–36
    approaches to educational leadership in, 36
Berkeley, B., 22
Billett, S., 64
Bingham, L. B., 50
Black Entertainment Television, 24
Blake, R.R., 45
Blanchard, K.H., 45
Boodhai, Navneet, 77

Boydell, T., 80
Bozalek, V., 74
Briton, D., 79
Brown, S., 52
Bryant, I., 79
Bryant, P., 52
bureaucratic organizations, 29
Burgoyne, J., 80
Burkus, D., 48
Byham, W., 45

Campion, M.A., 45
Caribbean colonies, 3
Caribbean Community, 9, 77
Caribbean culture, 3
Caribbean epistemologies, 11–12
Caribbean male, 22
Caribbean masculinity, 21
Caribbean societies, 3, 10, 100
caring leadership, 53
Carson, D.A., 17, 18
Carter, J. Adam, 14
Cartesian individualistic notion of "I," 17
Catholicism, 21
China: education system, 64–65
coherence, 18
collaboration, 49, 50
collaborative and cooperative skills, 50
collective consciousness, 10–11
communalism, 15
community building, 73–74

Conley, D.T., 45, 82
constructivism, 14, 19
Coopey, J., 80, 81
critical thinking, 15, 46–47, 49, 61, 63
critiquing, 61–62
Cusimano, J., 45

Da Costa, J.L., 83
decadence, notion of, 4
decline, notion of, 4
democracy, 3
democratic socialism, 15
deontology, 59
deschooling society, 73
dualism, 14
Duberley, J., 16
Durkheim, E., 19

educational leadership, 7
    in behavioural science era, 36
    imperatives of, 10–12
    in post-behavioural science era, 38
    in post-modern era, 97–98
    reimagination of, 8–10
    relevance of postmodernism and
        Proposition MRM for, 8–9
educational supervision, 90–92
education officer, as management
    consultant, 93–96
Edwards, R., 80
emotional intelligence (EQ), 51, 84
empiricism, 14
established narratives, notion of, 14–16

Facebook, 24
Farkas, C.M., 85
Fayol, H., 28–29, 45–46
#FeesMustFall, 74
feminism, 15, 22
Fong Foo, S., 52
Foster, W.P., 37, 91
Foucault, Michael, 18
Freire, P., 73
    theory of pedagogy, 73

fundamentalism, 13–14
fundamentalist thinking, 17
fundamentalist world view, 88

Garratt, B., 80
Geofroy, S., 22
Glanz, J., 84
Glass, R.D., 73
globalization, 14
gnawing pessimism, 17
Goldman, P., 45, 82
Goleman, D., 51, 84
Google, 24
Gordon, S.P., 37, 45
grand theory, 18–19, 28
Grenz, S., 17
Grogan, M., 15
Growe, R., 49
Gulick, L., 28–29

Habermas, Jurgen, 4
Hallinger, P., 45, 82
Harvey, D., 13
Hecht, B., 50
Heck, R., 82
hermeneutics, 20
Hersey, P., 45
Herzberg, F.I., 31
Hibbert Lectures, 19
Hoy, W.K., 18
human relations theory, 30–32, 45

idealism, 14
Illich, I., 73
inclusivity, 10–11
International Monetary Fund (IMF),
    56

Jacobson, B., 53
Jamaica, 3, 22–23, 31, 74
    civil service in, 3
    education system, 90
    Vision 2030, 92
James, William, 19

Japanese managers, 31–32, 44
Johnson, P., 16
Johnston, R., 79
Jules, D., 75

Kahn, W.A., 48
Kant, Immanuel, 60
Kaye, B., 53
Keunzli, A., 19, 25, 72
Keunzli-Monard, F., 19, 25, 72
Knitter, P.F., 19
knowledge, 20, 80
    commoditization of, 73
    consultant's body of, 93
Kocolowski, M.D., 44

Labelle, R., 65
Lai, E.R., 47
Lang, P., 82
leadership, 24–25, 27, 57, 100
    behavioural science approach, 36
    caring, 53
    in cooperative systems, 30
    local, 37
    in postmodern times, 81, 83
    servant, 52
    shared, 36
    theories of, 30–32
    transformational, 53
    transformational classroom, 89
liberal feminists, 22
Lin, T.B., 52
Lincoln, Abraham, 52
logical positivism, 14
long-term thinking, 71–72
Lyotard, Jean-François, 13, 18

macho West Indian male image, 23
maintenance of morale, 31
management consulting, 92–93
Manley, Michael, 5, 9, 10, 31, 100
    Up the Down Escalator, 56
    A Voice at the Workplace, 56
Manz, C.C., 44

Marcoulides, G.A., 82
Marxism, 18
Mayo, E., 30, 45, 72
McCullum, D., 79
McGregor, D., 31, 53
Medsker, G.J., 45
metanarratives, 15
Miller, E.L., 23
    theory of place, 23, 87
Miskel, C. G., 18
modelling, 60
modernism, 14
modernist educational approaches, 79
modernist thinking, 14
modernity, 3, 4
Moreno, A.P., 73
Morris, H.A., 65, 66
motivation, 61
motivational leadership, 71
Mouton, J.S., 45
multiculturalism, 22
Murphy, J., 37, 83

National Technical Qualifications
    Act, 77
Nettleford, Rex, 5, 9, 10, 55, 100
    Mirror Mirror, 55
Neville, R. F., 84
Nike, 24
Nokia, 24

O'Leary, R., 50
organizational leadership, 16, 26
organizational learning, 80
Organization for Economic Cooperation
    and Development (OECD), 68
Ouchi, W., 31–32, 44, 45, 53, 54, 88–89

Padgett, A.G., 18
Papper, E.M., 45
Parry, Odette, 22
participatory decision making, 32
Pearce, C.L., 44
Pedler, M., 80

Pescuric, A., 45
Peters, T., 45, 80
Phillips, A., 22
A Pluralist Universe, 19
Poplin, M.S., 45
Porath, C., 61
post-behavioural science era, 37–38
    approaches to educational leadership in, 38
postmodernism, 2, 4, 7, 8, 10, 13, 27, 99, 101
    age of, 14
    Caribbean and, 21–24
    challenges to "established" narratives, 14–16
    as a cultural phenomenon, 13
    feminism and, 22
    as a form of advocacy, 18
    negative criticisms of, 20
    as pessimism, 17
    phases of development, 21
    postmodern epistemology, 16–20
    shared learning and, 16
    social media and, 24–26
    view as a new era, 20–21
power, postmodern construction of, 25
power sharing, 44, 48
premodern era, 14, 17
principal as role model, 41
principals
    in modern Caribbean, 82–86
    role in postmodern era, 84–85
Proposition CJC, 53
Proposition MRM, 1, 6, 7–9, 38, 39–41, 100
    application of three interrogatives, 43
    Caribbean tomorrow and, 86–90
    as ethical construct, 59–61
    factors of, 42
    as framework for collaboration, 49–52
    as framework for long-term thinking, 71–72
    as justification for students' voices, 72–75
    as model of critical thinking, 47–49
    as pedagogical construct, 61–63
    philosophies of selected Caribbean thinkers, 54–57
    power sharing and, 44–47
    sustainable development (SD) and, 8, 50, 64, 68–71
    technical and vocational education and training (TVET) and, 63–71, 75–77
    vs other leadership theories, 52–54
public education, 3

Ramphal, Sir Shridath, 5, 9, 10, 11, 23, 54–55, 100
rationalism, 14
Ratnata, I.W., 75
Reese, M., 37, 45
regional integration, 55
reimagination of educational leadership, 8–10
relativism, 14
religious thought and life, 19
respect, 60, 63
Revisiting Global Trends in TVET: Reflections on Theory and Practice, 66
Robertson, R., 20–21
    Globalization, Social Theory and Global Culture, 20
rule utilitarianism, 59–60

scarcity, 65–66
Schein, E., 80
school supervision, 92–96
scientific management era, 28–29
    educational leadership in, 29–30
scientific methodology, 14
Senge, P., 80
Sergiovanni, T.J., 45, 81
servant leadership, 52
Shakib, Khosravi, 13
shared leadership, 36
Sheppard, B., 45
Simiyu, John W., 76
Simon, H.A., 45
Sloan, Alfred P., 48

social constructivism, 19–20
socialist feminists, 22
social media, 24–26
social phenomenon, 21
Southeast Asian economies, 65–66
structuralism, 18
struggle-for-hegemony phase, 21
#StudentBlackOut, 74
student-led protest movements, 74
sugar plantation economy, 3
Sustainable Development: Critical Issues, 68
sustainable development (SD), 8, 50, 64, 68–71
Sweet, R., 64

Taylor, E.W., 53
Taylor, Frederick, 28
technical and vocational education and training (TVET), 8, 63–71, 75–77
    in Kenya, 76
    in Papua New Guinea, 76–77
    "Strategy to Revitalize TVET in Africa," 77
tertiary educational institutions, 16
tertiary level of education, 16
Tester, K., 20
Theory X, 45
Theory Y, 31, 45, 53
Theory Z, 32, 54, 89
Thompson, C.S., 1–3, 5, 22, 44, 87, 88, 99–101
Tikly, L., 76
total quality management (TQM), 16, 48

Towards Solutions: Fundamentals of Transformational Leadership in a Postmodern Era, 8
transformational classroom leadership, 89
transformational leadership, 53
transition, notion of, 4
truth, 14, 17, 18

ubuntu principle, 17
UNESCO, 66–67, 76
Urwick, L., 28–29
Usher, R., 79, 80
utilitarianism, 59

Varieties of Religious Experience, 19
Vygotsky, L., 16, 73

Wanzare, Z., 83
Wassenaar, C.L., 44
Watermann, R.H., 45
Weber, M., 29, 45
Wetlaufer, S., 85
Winch, C., 75
Wittgenstein, Ludwig, 18
Wood, A.W., 63
Workers Vocational Skills Development Act, 77
World Bank, 56

Zembylas, M., 74
Zhang, Y., 52

www.ingramcontent.com/pod-product-compliance
Lightning Source LLC
Chambersburg PA
CBHW021833300426
44114CB00009BA/430